AWAKEN TO
THE WISDOM OF YOUR DREAMS

MIRRORS IN THE RIVER

Kathleen Duffy

Kathleen Duffy was reared in Lanmore, Westport, Mayo, Ireland. She now lives and works in Castlebar, Mayo. Known in Ireland for her popular workshops on Dream Wisdom, Kathleen Duffy works as a psychotherapist in private practice. She has also worked with the Tivoli Institute in Dublin. She has a particular interest in exploring the psyche through dreams as well as relationship issues and the transpersonal.

AWAKEN TO
THE WISDOM OF YOUR DREAMS

MIRRORS IN THE RIVER

Kathleen Duffy

To Patsy with Best wishe to many great & wonder day Dreams to be made manifest. Blessings, Kathleen Duffy

Covie Publications & Recordings

Published by Covie Publications and Recordings (CPR)
Sheeaune, Westport, Mayo, Ireland.
liamymac@gmail.com

CPR

ISBN 9780954574093

All Bible quotations taken from *The Jerusulem Bible*
© 1966 By Darton Longman & Todd Limited and Doubleday and Company Ltd.

All names in the book have been changed to protect identities.

Cover Illustration & Layout: Pat Tracey
www.Handeyestudios.com

AMDG

Dedicated to the memory of my parents
and their forebears and all who supported the nurturing
of the dreams brought to fruition with this book.

In order to remember your dreams
you will first need to *want* to remember them.
We do not forget what we consider to be important.

If you have this book in your hand,
you have already come some way on your journey
and are already open or willing to become open
to new challenges from within your self.

Contents

Appendices

Foreword

Those of us who are open to and curious about the wisdom stored in dreams will feel befriended by this book. It was Freud who said that the dream is "the royal road to the unconscious" and there are numerous texts which offer a familiar, strongly Freudian approach. This book is different.

Kathleen Duffy's approach is more eclectic and creative. She shows an openness to a range of meanings and layers of insight contained in dreams. She is not afraid to deploy ideas like 'soul' and 'spirit' when she deems it appropriate. She is not afraid to take the road, which to her, the dream signposts.

It's possible that some modern readers will find the notion of 'soul' disturbing and best kept safe in unvisited locked churches. If so, they will benefit all the more from the challenge this text offers. What disturbs us most is often what we most need.

In this book, psychotherapist Kathleen Duffy, undaunted, takes the 'soul' out of its reservation in crumbling protected structures on the margins of our lives and places it firmly where she knows it belongs.

For Kathleen, the soul speaks to us through dreams in the language of symbol. We can choose to ignore these messages and insist on living the 'rational' life in the 'rational' world. We can choose to live without the awareness of mystery or of its first cousin, the sacred.

On the other hand, we can adopt Kathleen Duffy as a guide to our own inner richness and imaginative possessions. Her work, which she shares with us in an inspiring and personal way, is as much about the business of 'soul-making' as it is about the process of psychotherapy.

Of course dreams can also assist in the more traditional psychotherapeutic tasks. They can help in the Psyche's attempt to renegotiate old injuries from the perspective of firmer and wiser ground. They can help us to heal.

Kathleen Duffy demonstrates, in numerous examples, how she allows her attention to 'float free' among the telling detail of the dream, linking the consciously known to the unconsciously intuited, finding a more expansive and creative way to broach and live with the injuries of personal history.

There is a generosity of spirit and warmth in this text along with a rare clarity. Readers will find a sense of connection and of possibility and will be inspired to discover their own unique path. All that readers will need to bring, as always, is the courage to begin.

Edward Boyne
Skyros

Chapter One

To Awaken, We Must First Remember

There are some wiser
In their sleeping
Than in their waking.
Olive Schreiner, *The Story of an African Farm*

God speaks first in one way, and then in another, but no one notices.
He speaks by dreams, and visions that come in the night, when
slumber comes on mankind, and men are all asleep in bed. Then it
is he whispers in the ear of man...
Job 33:14-16

Each dream has a hidden message or moral that is intimately related to our life, like any fairy tale, myth or legend, coming directly to us, about us, for us, from our soul. Our souls seek wholeness. While we sleep, whatever aspects of ourselves we have ignored, and whatever aspects of reality we have seen but chosen not to see, come to find us. Our dreams come from our largest selves, what we truly know, unlimited by the aims and fears of our smaller goals and anxieties.

Dreams are bringers of transcendent guidance, taking us beyond our egos and their narrow objectives. In the Biblical Book of Numbers, dreams are vividly described as the 'dark speech of the spirit.' Here we have a bridge between the spirit world and our conscious mind. In the scripture and myths of all traditions, great queens and humble shepherds alike receive their guidance from dreams. They might have been ordinary people living humdrum lives then they heed their dreams and go out in search of their unique destinies. Or perhaps they and their peoples were in dreadful predicaments from which there seemed no way out. They would heed their dreams and see a way to freedom and fruitfulness, though taking the steps involved might take great courage. All these 'stories' reflect an inner reality that is still true today. We still dream.

What a powerful guiding force!

From birth to death, we struggle to deal with the challenges, decisions and directions we must choose to give shape and meaning to our lives. As children, we look to our parents and the other adults around us. Later, we turn to teachers and peers for guidance. This guidance we rely on is influenced by the wider community and often, by religious structures. Yet the authorities from which we seek guidance and direction are often restricted in one way or another by their own experiences. Without consciously knowing what they do, they pass on and reconstruct their limiting beliefs. These limitations easily enter our Psyches and become our own.

With modern technology at our fingertips, we have access to all sorts of global information. We have reached the moon and other planets and are looking for still more knowledge. Yet, even as we expand our search in the outer dimension, we run the risk of moving further away from the rich, inner wisdom that is freely available to us, coming nightly from our souls via our dreams.

If this profound source of wisdom is available to us, why do we spend so much of our time looking outside of ourselves for guidance?

The realisation of dreams is often closer than we believe. Consider the following tale, known in many traditions, and recently retold to me by a friend in Wexford:

A little over seventy years ago I accompanied my father to an auction on a farm in a place called Sceachmolan not far from Murrintown in the parish of Piercestown. We travelled by horse and cart. As we journeyed, along my father told me this story about Sceachmolan and the family who lived there.

In my father's young days two old men lived there called Michael and John. As a young man, John began having a strange dream which suggested that if he stood on the middle of the Bridge of London he would find his fortune. Although John told some neighbours and friends about this troubling dream, it would not leave him, contrary to the old belief. They thought he was going round the bend. He hated going to bed so he walked the roads until sheer tiredness drove him to seek some rest. Still the dream kept coming back.

The years went by. John was now over forty and poor, with a small farm. At the fair in Wexford, he met my father's uncle, Martin, who bought two small cattle from him and listened to his dream.

Martin pondered for a while before encouraging John to follow his dream. Since John had never travelled, never been on a train, nor even been in a city, this was a daunting journey, but he went.

As directed, he stood on the middle of the bridge. After doing this for five days he said to himself, "If nothing happens tomorrow I'm going home."

On the sixth day he was looking down into the river when a man tapped him on the shoulder to ask him if he was looking for something.

John eyed the stranger up and down before telling him his story.

The stranger laughed and said in reply: "My good man, forget about your dream and go home. All my life I've been dreaming about a place in Ireland called Sceachmolan and how, if I dug under an apple tree in the bottom of the garden, there I would find a crock of gold." Taking a few steps away, the stranger turned and said, "The tree is on its own just by the fence."

John hurried off the bridge, and collecting his few belongings, headed for home. He knew this tree well for it was in his own orchard.

Back in Sceachmolan, he got the spade and began to dig around and under the apple tree until he found an earthenware crock. The crock could hold about a gallon of water and it had a lid with a grab handle in the middle. Inside he found a considerable number of gold sovereigns.

John lived well for a few years but the gold was soon spent and he was poor again. He often looked at the crock, which he now used for holding water, and he wondered what this strange writing on the inside of it might mean.

John was sitting by his fire one day when a travelling man came in. He gave him a mug of tea, and as they chatted, the traveller was looking at the crock on the dresser.

"Can you read that?" asked John.

The traveller examined the strange writing on the inside of the crock. "Yes," he replied. "It says 'faoin ceann seo, tá ceann eile,' under this one, there is another."

John could hardly wait for the traveller to leave. Sure enough he found another crock at a deeper level, which left him rich once again.

It was at that auction all those years ago, in the company of my father, that I saw the same crock sold for the sum of a pound. I was a small boy then and a pound was a pound.

When I heard this tale I was reminded of the message of Christ when He spoke of the Kingdom of Heaven being hidden in the human heart. The wisdom of this story remains universal, whatever its origin. I have come across similar versions both in Jewish and Portuguese-language (via Paulo Coelho) literature. The important point remains the same - the dreamer is called forth out of smallness to follow a calling. And the tale challenges us all to meet and encounter our fears in unknown territory. We must go through the emotions of feeling foolish as we develop patience and endurance. And we must risk opening up to strangers, revealing rather than hiding our dream of hope.

The story is rich in symbolism, starting with the calling from that same place of mystery we shall return to often in these pages. There is resistance. Young John tries to offload the responsibility he feels to follow his dream. He tries, following local belief, to 'make it go away' by telling friends and neighbours about the vision, but to no avail. How often do we try to make recurrent calls to responsibility go away?

Interesting too that it is while travelling to an auction with his father that the boy-narrator is entrusted with this story. Going to an auction, a place of exchange, like the Fair where John ultimately gets the encouragement he needs to take action. A Fair is where we barter and give what we have to offer to receive what we need. A Fair Day is also a space where tradition is handed down and new deals are made, a place of mingling and integration where young men and women are inducted in the next stage of their development. Thus the young man meets his uncle, symbol of the wise man, who thinks deeply before offering guidance to the young seeker.

The bridge, a symbol of transition, is a most interesting feature. A bridge is a structure that connects two worlds and water flows underneath. When John looks into the river, you could say he was reflecting on the flow of his own life. Water is the necessary symbol for all life and also the symbol of the unconscious realm (a notion we shall return to in the pages that follow).

John must learn to cope with his thoughts and feelings here on this bridge as he tries, in vain, to pass unnoticed. In other tellings, notably by Rumi, it is a policeman, symbol of order and authority, who connects with him. Faced with an outer authority, the seeker returns to inner riches. Each mirrors the other in their experience of their dreams.

The 'crock' is known to be a vessel or container of gold. Remember that gold is the most valuable of metals, refined by fire before it is stamped for trading as gold. In a similar way we all must go through the process and fires of change, through challenge and purification before we become pure in nature. We all know someone who has a 'heart of gold' i.e., someone able to love purely.

Before the seeker sets out on his journey to the local marketplace, he has already grappled for years with his dilemma. He has risked being ridiculed and written off as mad when he shared his dream. Yet he continued to share, first with the uncle from whom he took counsel and later with that stranger in London who told him to go home.

It was in his returning to the place from whence he came, Sceachmolan, that he discovered his treasure. Note that the back garden (we see this motif return later in 'The Scream' transcript) is more private, unlike the front, which is on display and representative of ego. It is in this place, synonymous with the self, that the seeker finds a buried resource to sustain himself. Even here we learn that, whilst we can be appeased for a while by the illusion that gold meets our needs, we become poor again, and poor in spirit if we settle for the riches gold has to offer.

We need to dig deeper into the 'soil' of self to find the deeper treasures. It is interesting to discover that the writing was not displayed on the outside, but hidden on the inside of the crock, reserved for those who choose to investigate the inner world!

Note also that the quest ends under an apple tree, well known symbolically from the Biblical story of Creation and Awakening and known there as the Tree of Knowledge. When the woman eats from the apple her eyes are opened. Eve then brought Adam into consciousness by having him eat and be awakened too.

Life will continue to challenge us to go out into the world of our discomfort as well as to return to our inner world to dig and delve ever deeper for our own hidden messages and treasures. It is not only by becoming a traveller but also by welcoming our fellow traveller into our heart and home that we become enlightened. And hopefully become the traveller who will be able to read the strange words written on the inside of the hearts of future dreamers.

******

The following transcript was instrumental in the completion of this book. You too may find friends and supporters have comparable dreams to help you on your way. My friend Angela sent me the following transcript.

Dream: The Word Pool

I am in a large room. It is peaceful, beautiful, almost all white with bits of lush green plants, palms, and orchids of every size and colour sort of coming out of every surface. There is minimal furniture in the room, but what is there is white. A table. Three chairs. And some of those rice paper room dividers, but not seeming to block off anything really, just there. There are lots of windows and doors, some big, some small. Most, but not all, are slightly opened, and the most amazing golden light is shining in. It is warm, and sparkly and moving in and around the room, in and around me.

Then I notice that running kind of through the middle of the room, but slightly to the right, is a stream of water, filled with the most incredible river stones and brilliant gemstones, and there is a light at the bottom of the stream that is shining up through the stones and gems; and that coming into the room, being carried by this blue-green water, are these words (not on paper, not in or on anything),

14

just gliding along on the top of the rippling water as though they are being carried somewhere.

At the other end of this vast room, there is a collecting pool. The water gently cascades from the floor into this pool, and all of the words are moving about inside the pool. I am trying to figure out what these words are, why they are there and what they mean.

I pick up some of the words, and I can see that these are words from your book - dreams, gift, Scripture (those are the only three that I recall now, but there were so many at the time. I wish I could remember more). I knew right away that it was all of the words from your writing, from your book.

Then, you are there, only you are bigger, bigger than ever. And I don't mean fat or anything, just you, only bigger (kind of like an Alice in Wonderland kind of bigger). And you start picking these words up and out of the sparkling pool, and you are so excited. You are dancing around and giggling and filled with nothing short of glee. This seems to go on for some time. Then there is a knock at the door.

Then the dream shifts, and I am at another place, holding this big box filled with all of these words and I can feel the words moving around inside the box, not like moving place per se, but vibrating would be more like it.

Yes, that's it. It's like the box has a pulse, and it is a fast pulse. And I am to meet with this counsel of people to bring them this pulsating box. I remember feeling shy because it was all so much bigger than anything I could imagine. I say to them that I have brought this box for them. I walk up these wide, expansive marble-like stairs (white marble with golden flecks) to take the box to them. My hands are shaking. My heart is pounding almost now as fast as the pulsating of the words inside the box. I get to the top of the stairs where they are sitting, and I place the box on a table.

One person of the counsel comes to the box and asks me to open it. I tell her/him (I can't remember which it was), that I can't, that he or she has to open it. He or she touches the box, and it is like the box dissolves and all of the words are just there, without this container now...and then that golden light from earlier in the dream is everywhere and it goes off like fireworks inside the room...and then I wake up. I wanted so badly to be back in the dream to see what happened next. But that was it. It was finished.

******

The Secret Language of the Soul

One reason that we do not heed our dreams is that they speak to us in a quite different language from the one we are used to. They speak in the rich, ancient language of symbol and ritual, a language that has largely been lost over the past centuries of our modern, industrialised civilization. We retain fewer and fewer outward ceremonies of the Psyche and the sacred whereby great collective truths were once transmitted. We are in some ways the poorer for it. But we do have our dreams, a source of ritual that takes place in our Psyche each night.

It took the great 20th century pioneers of psychology and anthropology, such as Freud, Carl Jung, Károly Kerényi and Marie-Louise von Franz to show that the language of symbol is in fact still very much alive. Only now, it lives within us. They pointed to the many parallels between the ancient rituals of diverse cultures and the ways in which our dreams speak.

The language of dream, of symbol and image, and irrational experience, is by its very nature alien to our rational mind. Rational mind speaks about what it can explain and understand. Unconscious mind, with laws of its own, speaks through experience, often as initially bewildering as it is intense.

The cloud of non-sense and mystery surrounding every dream does not mean that we cannot learn to find our way in them. This book is an attempt to show, by example as much as explanation, how we can learn to awaken to the meaning and significance of our dreams, even, or especially, the ones that seem crazy, nonsensical, embarrassing, or trivial.

We will not 'translate' the language of dreams. There can be no rigid dictionary of dreaming. The dream world manages always to be both archetypal and highly personal, composed as they are of the raw material of our lives. We can learn to truly 'feel our way' into their particular meanings for us. In this way their wise guidance can begin to operate in our daily lives.

Remembering Dreams

To begin to work with your dreams, you must first have access to them.

Many people turn away from their dreams, feeling they are just 'too crazy.' Others come to believe they do not dream at all. Most know that they dream, catching an occasional glimpse, a profound change in mood, but seldom, if ever, really remember with any certainty.

I know from working with many such people that these conditions change radically, with a certain understanding. It is not our lack of mental capacity that blocks us from remembering our dreams or other events in our life. Memory plays a major role on the journey from unconscious to conscious. It is a defensive part of ourselves, which chooses to block out that which we consider to be negative, unpleasant or not important. To listen to what our unconscious has to say can be painful and will challenge us to change and grow. It will show us our blind spots, even using people who are visually impaired or blind in our dreams to awaken us to this message.

It is important to examine our attitudes to the events we forget. We might have an unspoken desire to resist 'showing up' for them. We would rather not know. When we 'show up,' we are required to take responsibility for our presence and actions. We can offer many seemingly legitimate reasons not to pay attention to our dreams. We are too tired.

They make no sense, or take too much valuable time. But it is important to note what we might be avoiding. When we are prepared to accept that our dreams give voice to the Psyche seeking wholeness, that every soul longs to be reunited with its full potential, then doors can begin to open.

In order to remember your dreams you will first need to *want* to remember them. We do not forget what we consider to be important. If you have this book in your hand, you have already come some way on your journey and are already open or willing to become open to new challenges from within your self.

Here are some of the suggestions, and the reasons for them, that I use to help my clients and pupils remember their dreams:

1. Before going to sleep, offer an intention to be attentive to your waking. This means both being attentive to what you experience on waking from a dream and being attentive to your dreams and the wisdom they present. Linger with your eyes closed in that place between the worlds of sleep and being awake for a brief moment both before falling asleep and as you wake up.

And if there is a situation about which you are particularly anxious, or about which you need more clarity, ask your soul for guidance. In this way, while that gatekeeper, your ego, is off-duty during sleep, your dream wisdom can find its way. This is where we submit the raw material of our day to the masters of sleep.

2. When you wake, linger at the moment between sleeping and waking.

This moment of waking is where the dream is to be encountered. It is the threshold between what can seem to be two very different realities. Yet when you begin to explore, you will find they are very linked.

Before you look at the clock, or open your eyes to any distraction or calling from the outside world, stay in this elusive space for a brief moment to retrieve the rich harvest of your night's sleep. It is best not to wake up to an alarm or radio. The sudden intrusion can jolt you out of the dream state and thrust you into the conscious world with the effect of shutting a door on all that was coming through to consciousness from within. **Make an effort to recall what you have just experienced and note what you are feeling.** Try to resist the regressive pull of falling back to sleep. Honour the struggle to become conscious of any glimpse or message from your soul, as you would watch for a message or sign from an eager lover.

3. In a notebook kept beside your bed write down your dream exactly as you recall it paying attention to as much detail as you can.

In dreams, nothing is without significance. Pay attention to all the detail the dream has presented, just as it is presented. Sometimes you may even want to draw what you have 'seen' or paint it later on. The temptation will be to ignore the parts you do not like to think have anything to do with you. Trust the wisdom that the dreamer within you has for choosing all aspects. If all were in order, we would not need to dream.

In Daniel 7:1 we note that Daniel "had a dream and visions that passed through his head as he lay in bed. He **wrote the dream down...**"

4. At first, make no attempt to understand or analyse your dream.
Just present the dream to paper, and note the impact it has simply on your feelings. Later you can begin to work with the dream content and engage your mind with the business of understanding its message.

5. It is important to note in particular the opening scene or place where your dream takes place.

This will inform you about the context and time to which your dream relates. All other content will have relevance once context is established. For example, the opening dream scene might be from your childhood, or someplace familiar from some earlier experience, or indeed from a place recently visited.

At first you might not have any idea about why this particular place is featured. And yet when you, the dreamer, let yourself spontaneously visit your most recent memory or experience of being in that place, house or room, shop or church, car or train, garden or forest, you will find that it holds a message.

The essence of your experience of that place might now be playing out in another area of your life. Your dream is calling your attention to exactly what the experience of that place evokes in you.

6. The final scene and especially the energy or feeling at the point where we wake up is most important to note.

This is usually the place where we are challenged to face some fear. This points us in the direction of our next challenge. It is usually at the point of most fear or challenge that we wake up to avoid the pain. For example, we might wake up just at the point where the person chasing us is about to catch up with us and perhaps reveal his/her identity. The dream invitation would be to face that which we are running away from. In my own situation the person chasing me might be someone who has already published a book while I still run from such a challenge! Ask yourself, "If I did not wake up at that moment, what would I have had to face?"

This information, or insight, will lead you to where you need to place your attention.

7. Scan the day or days prior to the dream for clues as to what the dream is trying to help you with.

Ask yourself what emotional or mental energy you took to sleep with you. It is out of this energy that the dream draws its images. It is as if your inner nightshift of workers is at the ready to create a personal documentary about the situation of your life. Your soul is the director.

8. Try not to be selective about which dreams you write down.

It is important to give attention to them all as equally important. Dreams bring us the full story. Ego is selective about what it reveals. It is that which we have not fully integrated, what we have ignored, suppressed, avoided, or is about to challenge us that our dreams offer us.

9. Note patterns or repeated symbols in your dreams.

You might, for example, have many dreams in which a particular person recurs. Or perhaps it is a building or landscape. Such 'clues' are important, and may be quite subtle. A woman I worked with had several dreams in which, although the settings varied and different people appeared, the anxious feeling conveyed was always the same. Looking closer, we saw there was after all, a recurring pattern. It was colour. The colours green and yellow always appeared quite vividly, in one dream on a car, in another a building, in yet another on a piece of clothing.

At length the dreamer remembered that green and yellow were the colours of her school uniform as a child. Now everything could begin to make sense regarding the many dreams in which these colours strongly appeared. A particular and very difficult feeling she experienced while in school was being highlighted in all the various, ostensibly present-day situations in her dreams.

It is typical of the language of dreams that the woman did not simply dream of her school and what took place there. The ego will not want to revisit any place or situation of pain, which it has decided to bury or suppress. Any direct link to a place of pain will be denied access. Dream wisdom must therefore be subtle and clever enough to bypass the ego in allowing important information to come at length to consciousness.

It is only by paying attention to the 'smallest' details in each and every dream that we can awaken to what they tell us. This may sound impossible to those who feel that they never dream at all, or remember only the most vague of impressions. Yet it is extraordinary what will begin to come to consciousness once the intention is there.

I always ask my clients to tell me their dreams twice over, and on the second occasion, to include what they left out the first time. "I left nothing out!" they protest, but then they realise that they neglected to reveal at least one little, and, as it usually turns out, revealing detail. Often it might be that the action is recorded but not the emotional content, feeling, or mood.

The following dreams are all, in a sense, dreams about dreaming, calls from the Psyche that it is time to pay more attention to the life within. These are taken from my own dream journals and from my notes of dreams brought to me by friends and clients. Names have been changed in all. They are presented here as examples of a process that may be taken up by anyone wishing to awake to her or his dreams.

Chapter Two

Messages from the Soul

*While we might on some days prefer to simply be happy carrots,
relieved of our urgencies, our anxieties and impossible desires, we
also suffer greatly when we are not living the life which the Psyche
wishes us to live. Such existential bad faith will always demand
some payment, in the body, in our relationships, in our disturbing
dreams, or in the burden our children will have to carry for us.*
James Hollis, *On This Journey We Call Our Life*

Dream: Life at a Deeper Level

*I am working in the bog, spreading turf (peat), when I notice a new
cut. It leads up to an area of the bog that has not been cut or opened
before.*

*The turf is only cut from the top few sods and I feel there are walls
at a deeper level, like the Céide Fields in north Mayo a renowned
stone-age archaeological site.*

*I know this because of the instrument I am using. I feel the evidence
of a deeper foundation below as I send down an iron bar.*

*I am wondering, as I usually did as a child, about this older life that
went on before and that somehow got covered over and buried. I do
not know how deep it is, only that it is at a much deeper level than
we are working at. This part of the bog is new to work in.*

Reflection: For as long as I can remember I have been interested in
old ruins and the stories they might tell of the lives they once sheltered
before they fell down and were covered in ivy or buried. But the
curiosity I experienced in this dream is clearly not only about the life
that was buried in the bog. It is also about what was covered and
buried in my own childhood.

In this dream, whatever evidence there is below the surface is reachable because of the instrument I am using, the strong iron bar. This tool could also be described as dreamwork. It is what I use to uncover, expose and shed the light of consciousness on unconscious content, to highlight and heal original wounds.

Looking at the story of the Céide Fields in Mayo, from which this dream takes its image, I remember Séamus Caulfield. It was he, who, as a young boy, was aware that his father had discovered walls of stone deep in the bog. These walls were the first evidence of an ancient civilisation, a community that had lived there over five thousand years ago. Séamus Caulfield grew up to become the archaeologist, who uncovered and explored this site that forever changed perceptions of Irish landscape and history, shedding light on an ancient buried way of life.

Vital, valuable information from our earliest experience, of how we first made sense of life, can be lost, unless we have the courage of our curiosity and a strong tool to work with. We can allow our original spontaneity to be covered over by the conditioning of our parents, peers, teachers and culture at the time when we are at our most vulnerable. But this can be regained and change the way we meet the world. I took this dream as encouragement to use the dream work to look deeper into my own past and see what new vistas might open.

Constance Rubini and Frederic Bodet, the authors of *The Little Book of Miró,* describe how the Spanish artist Joan Miró despised stagnation and hovered for inspiration between nature and 'an inner dream world.' Although Miró was naturally drawn to drawing as a child, his father (a prosperous businessman) registered him in business school. Young Joan would have been in his natural element and literally *drawing* (to pun on that word) from his right creative brain as a child, but in business classes, he was shaped to develop his left (or more rational) brain. Later, while confined to the world of transactions and accounts, his psychological distress was such that he fell ill. He subsequently decided to devote his life to painting and was tutored by Francisco Gali who sensitised his students to poetry and music (right brain activity).

The mature Miró divided his time between the city (Paris, Barcelona) and the countryside (his native Catalonia). His desire to connect with the social and artistic life of Paris as well as a desire to keep to himself caused some suffering, and he struggled for a way to respect both aspects of himself. The solution came in his work. He describes his famous painting *The Farm* as "a résumé of my entire life in the country" into which he "put everything I loved about the country... from a huge tree to a tiny snail."

Miró also describes how he spent hours and hours making an ant come alive. It is as if he had reconnected with the natural childlike quality of being totally engrossed in what he was doing. He said that while he was working on *The Farm* (for up to seven or eight hours a day) he suffered greatly, like a condemned man, as he worked and reworked the paint in his attempt to get rid of "all those foreign influences" and in touch with his native soil. Miró too unearthed rich material from deep in the past. He was fascinated by cave paintings imbued with spirituality, mystery and magic.

Such openness to the dreamscape is common among artists. Vincent Van Gogh claimed a straightforward approach, "I dream my painting, then I paint my dream."

Consider the following dream and the painting which presented itself from the dream.

Dream: Butterfly Released

Tina finds herself back in the place of her painful childhood. There was a field nearby where she often went to find solace in the company of a lonely donkey. The field was sparse with grass, and no one, except the silent child, seemed to take heed or care of this neglected creature. He was tied to a stake, and she identified with his sense of restriction. The high walls round this field, topped by wire, mirrored the walls she felt she needed to build round her young and very sensitive heart.

Whilst she feels the bleakness again of her childhood, Tina now has the company of her therapist (me). I encourage her to open her hands, which are tightly clutching something. As I place my hands under hers for support, she sees a butterfly emerging, wings aflutter, to fly from her palm. When she opens her eyes she finds a meadow of colourful flowers in a place once barren and full of darkness.

Reflection: Tina painted the image. The butterfly symbolises the transformation of her Psyche. She too was emerging from a dark chrysalis, her own past. Tina's wounded heart was opening up to her creativity as she painted many of the nightmares and, in therapy, was able to utter some of the darkness of her past.

The butterfly is but one instance. We often associate different creatures with various human behaviours and emotions. For example, the fox is noted for slyness, the chicken for fear, the hare for speed, the rabbit for softness, the bull for rage, and the snail for slowness.

******

This next dream came after spending a night at Christmas time in my childhood home.

Dream: The Drowsy Elephant

I notice an Animal that first seems like a horse, but then seems to have become an elephant. The Animal's two front feet are tied together and it is pleading with me to set it free. I feel bad for it and am moved as I explain that someone is coming soon to set it free. The elephant now slumps over on one side, as if in prison, and tries to go to sleep. Now he is coming towards me, and I am kissing him as I wake up feeling aroused.

Reflection: Many memories were triggered here as I slept in the place where these memories were once lived and experienced. Animals in our dreams can represent our instinctual nature. Being curious about the Psyche's choice of detail, I wondered why the Animal was an elephant, as opposed to any of the farm Animals I would have been familiar with. The association that 'elephants never forget' drew my attention to all the memories I have 'tied up' with my childhood home. The bound feet prevent it going forward. In my waking life, the year ending also held a lot of tied-up emotions and memories that were about to be recreated in order to be healed. I am feeling compassion for the Animal as I negotiate the time until freedom. Kissing the elephant suggests an integration with instinct and there is an awakening of the senses as I wake in an aroused state.

Sleep is presented within the dream as a coping option before liberation. Asleep we enter an unconscious state, the realm of stored memories and unexpressed emotions. From this great storehouse, our Psyche presents us each night with images appropriate for a statement to our consciousness as we wake. Consider the *loyalty* of our Soul Self in its continual effort to have us face and embrace all of who we are. Looked at that way, I hope you can join me in saying: I love my Soul!

Dream: Marshy Ground

Ailish's dream was repeated five nights in a row.
Ailish experiences herself standing beside her house, one foot on solid ground and the other unable to take the necessary step to join her right foot because the space between them is marshy and swampy.

This is where she woke up each time.

Reflection: This short, insistent dream demonstrates how eager our Soul/Self is, to meet us with wisdom from the storehouse of our psychic history. It shows how determined it is to lead us towards an examined life, when we might have preferred to just live day to day.

This was the dream that brought Ailish to me. She did not know what it might have been about, but she realised that it must have been trying to tell her something important, since she dreamed it night after night. Ailish is a competent, intelligent woman. She had achieved a great deal in her professional life. In her marriage and private life, however, there was suffering, and she was at an impasse.

We began by exploring the setting of the dream. I asked her where she was standing. She said first that it was "just round the corner" from the back door of the house in which she lived. Looking closer, we were able to establish that this is a side of her home that she seldom used or even took notice of.

It is also the side of Ailish's house from which the ocean can be seen. The ocean is not visible from inside the house, only a bathroom window of opaque, frosted glass faced that way. But, she said, this closed-off side of the house was able to withstand the elements of the winds and storms that come off the sea.

When we explored her expression "round the corner," her description for the scene of the dream, she recognised the expression, "having turned the corner." To turn a corner is to enter new territory in life. To arrive at this place, where she did not normally go, she came through her back door.

It is Carl Jung's view that the house is most often a symbol of the self. From this perspective, we noted the significance of the front door being Ailish's usual way of coming and going. The 'front door' is the side we show the public but in the dream she uses the back door, the more private and least explored. And when she goes that way, when she 'turns the corner' what does she discover? She views the threatening yet magnificent ocean.

In depth psychology, poetry and mythology, the ocean is a symbol of our vast unconscious world. Ailish's 'house' is well protected from that place. It is in looking that way that Ailish experiences the 'sinking feeling' that frightened her when she awoke.

Staying with that sensation in the dream, we were able to recover a particular memory from her childhood when she was literally on such un-solid ground. Ailish had stepped into a bog hole, a quagmire into which people and large Animals can sink and suffocate. She remembered the 'sinking feeling' and her terror as she screamed out for help until her father came and rescued her. He assured her, as he came, that she would be alright.

In revisiting, through dream, that earlier trauma of being on un-solid ground, Ailish's Psyche was presenting her with a most accurate image of her present life. Her 'right foot' is on solid ground, and yet, she is afraid to bring her left foot to join it. We know that the right side of the brain concerns itself with all that is emotional, feminine, spiritual and irrational, and it governs the left side of the body. Conversely, the left side of the brain is the seat of the logical, focused and rational mind and it governs the right side of the body. Ailish was accomplished and secure in her male, logical, public world. This is depicted in her dream by having her right foot on solid ground. It was in her emotional, personal and private life that she was wounded and lost. The wisdom of her dream was showing her the image from her earlier experience that most accurately expressed the 'sinking feeling' of un-solid ground and of having to call out for help.

The dream told her two things: she needed to confront the deep ocean of soul experience from which she had hitherto averted her gaze and she needed to call for help. Now, the help she needed was a guide to help her through her own unconscious world, someone to lead her to where she could move forward in her emotional private life with the same confidence with which she moved through the rational public world. She brought her dream to me. And, just as her father had called out as he crossed the marsh toward her, I could assure her that she would 'be all right.'

Dream: Unsteady Foundation

Jane dreams about a woman in a hostel wearing two very different shoes, and they are on the wrong feet. One shoe has her two middle toes exposed and raised, while the other one is black with high heels.

Reflection: The location of the opening of a dream is always significant. Here the woman with the odd shoes is in a hostel. When I asked Jane, the dreamer, what a hostel meant to her, she said a hostel is a place where many people pass through. It offers temporary respite to pilgrims of life.

The woman's mismatched shoes and their being on the wrong feet, give the impression of a little girl wearing her mother's shoes, playing at being grown up. I explored with Jane what position she had in her family. She said that she was the middle child in a large family. She, with another sibling, both felt unseen. They were the 'middle toes,' she said.

In the dreamer's present situation, she saw her footing in life as very unsteady, as represented by her wearing the high heels. The challenge of the dream was to look at ways in which she might still be 'playing at being a grown-up' while actually acting childishly. One way she could see was the act of 'putting on a mask of adulthood,' affecting an appearance of invulnerability in her interaction with others, a mask which actually served to block true adult communication.

Did the image of the middle toes exposed and raised tell her she still felt squeezed out of place and not really grounded? Yes, as she had felt while being raised in this family. Note the use of the word 'raised' here. The dream gives the image to depict the experience! Was she still living as though that was the case, even though the circumstances had changed?

Jane saw that this was indeed the case. The dream was a demand from within to give herself respite, the space and attention in her present life that she had felt deprived of as a child. It was time for her to step into her own shoes.

Dream: The Sixth Message

A short, succinct dream: There is a message for me on my telephone answering machine, telling me that I had five messages, and now, I have six.

Reflection: This dream came to me at the time in my life when I was beginning to develop and trust my own intuition. I took the answering machine as a symbol of self, capable of sending and receiving messages. I had already been using all five senses, now my Psyche acknowledged that I had a sixth sense to attend to.

Incidentally, new channels from the Psyche can often be opened up by a life change in the world of conscious reality. According to Katarzyna Skonieczna, on her website *Terra Incognito*, the late Irish painter Tony O'Malley experienced a 'golden period' in his life and in his work after his marriage. "He virtually explodes with creativity, vitality and shine and so do the... paintings of the last decades of his life. He called them 'paradises,' 'dreams,' 'songs.' they adopt (a) startling exotic palette... and dancing, wonderfully fluid and free compositions made out of imaginative and abstracted elements." It strikes me that these same words could be equally used of the dreamscape. Katarzyna Skonieczna then goes on to praise O'Malley as "the painter of his own intimate, extremely deep - almost mystical relationship with the Earth and its energies."

Dream: The Felan Sisters

There is some sort of ritual or dance in the church. The Felan sisters are involved and I am to assist them in getting ready. They arrive wearing very ornate black and gold clothing. I am to sew the hem on the coat for one sister at two different levels. Each colour has its own level. We are pinning something together. One of the sisters is wearing a dress from my wardrobe, and I make some comment about the fact that all this is happening at the back of the church.

The Felan sisters are about to dance.

Reflection: The women in this dream, the Felan sisters, were creative, articulate and very capable and, as yet, teenage members of a family who lived near me for a period of my life in the 1980s. When I wondered why they appeared in my dream I realised their significance lay in their name, not even its spelling, but its sound. This is how dreams work. Everything is significant, even the sound of words. In my dream the Felans were to represent the feelings or feminine energies. This is amplified by the fact the dream showed me only the women of the Felan family. They represent the feminine, feeling aspect of the soul. I am helping them to get ready for a ritual with dance, which is about to happen in the church.

A dance can be seen as freedom of movement or liberation.

The location of the dream is the 'back of the church.' In either case, I notice that the dream takes place in 'the back' of the church, the place of preparation in ancient rituals before entry to the sacredness of the Mass. To understand what the Felans and I were preparing for (not properly in the church yet, but 'in the back,' just as the sisters are not fully developed at this time but in their teenage stage), I had to look, both literally and symbolically, at what was going on in the history of the Church at the time of the dream.

The struggle, then in the 1980s, was, as it still is, with the old, paternalistic structure that kept the role of the feminine out of the Roman Catholic Church. This exclusion existed in practical terms, as women were only accepted in subservient roles. It was also psychic as the church leaders shrank from the feminine aspects of the soul/ spiritual life.

There had been a strong movement towards inclusion in the Second Vatican Council in the early 1960s. That council upheld the forgotten, earlier scriptural teaching, that above and beyond the hierarchies of the Church, the "Holy Spirit distributes his grace among the faithful of every rank," (Lumen Gentium). Vatican II returned the charisms to doctrine. This meant giving validity to individual inner experience, vision and the irrational - the spirit speaking directly, as in dreams and visions. Since that time there had been considerable retreat into confining the spiritual life to the hierarchies of the church. In my dream I saw that spirit rising again. To me it showed the preparation for the entry of the feminine into the church.

I could see this dream very literally as my soul's commentary on movement within the ancient structure of the Catholic Church. Or I could see it describing as movement within the dreamer's (my own) Psyche in preparation for the liberation of the life of the feelings. I believe it was both.

It is always important to notice the 'task' of the dreamer. And once again the meaning is two-fold; the dream is speaking of the structure of the Church, as I would wish it to be and the structure of my inner 'church' or spirit. I am adjusting the ritual garments of the dancers. Ritual garments have great significance in the Church. To be a 'man of the cloth' was a well-known reference to the priesthood. The traditional dress was black. I was adjusting this garment with the two-layered hem of black and of gold. Black and gold are in such contrast to each other, like the stars in a black sky, offering glimpses of life at other levels. This is just what the church was being challenged to accept by the inclusion of the feminine. And this, perhaps, was my task in relation to the Church. I had a black and gold coat in my own wardrobe at the time. Was I perhaps being asked to take that creative balance out and put it to use?

It was the hem in particular that I was adjusting. I was reminded of the gospel story where a woman from the crowds, who had been subject to bleeding for twelve years came forth and touched the hem of His cloak. Jesus turned to her and said, "Courage my daughter, your faith has restored you to health." And from that moment the woman was well again. (Matt 9:20-22, Luke 8:43-48) I understood this story to be more about the faith of the woman than about the religious structure of the time. And the dream was surely about my own soul being healed, as much as that of the Church.

Dream: Valuables

Inside an old house I am peeling off layers of paint from a door. The different colours represent the number of layers that had been applied. I am managing well in getting the paint off and revealing the natural wood underneath.

At the top of the door I discover and uncover a garment. It had been thrown across the door and painted over, so that it had disappeared from sight. The garment comes easily away as I peel off the paint. I hold it in my hands and see that it is a loose dress, the kind we call a 'smock' and worn during pregnancy.

I look in the pockets of the smock and am excited to find gifts wrapped up. There are two separate boxes. I open them and find gold chains and lockets in perfect condition. Then I continue to find more things - two beautifully knitted dolls, and baby clothes. I give one of the dolls to my friend E. She is excited. I decide to keep one gift to give to my sister when her baby is born.

Now I am looking in other places. On the top of old wardrobes I am finding more valuables - pendants, rings, bracelets. They are all gold. Everywhere I find secret places to explore, behind the wallpaper or in tiny openings in the walls. And I keep finding more gifts. There are so many treasures yet to be found that I give more away to other friends.

I realise that these objects of value I am finding for my friends are the reason why I was always interested in these old places.

Then I find a picture of one of the girls who lived in this house in the past. She is wearing one of the rings I have just discovered.

*I feel strongly that **I have finally found what I was looking for.***

Reflection: I have always been curious about the layers of different coloured paint on walls, doors and furniture in old houses. Each layer represents the choice of the person who paints it at a given time. Then another colour or layer is added. It could be because the same person grew tired of it or perhaps the fashion of the day changed. Maybe someone new with a different desire came to make his or her own distinctive mark.

In this dream the layers of paint are the residues of all the different people who influenced me as I was growing up. If the door in this dream were to speak, it might say: "I have been coloured by many opinions or by the different opinions of many. Now, in the moment of the dream I am being seen at my original level. In this process I reveal sacred insight about life at an earlier stage."

Peeling off the layers of paint to reveal the original quality of the wood is not unlike the process of peeling back layers of personality to get to the quality of the core self. Blending in or becoming invisible is a well-known way of surviving certain circumstances when we are young.

The garment in the dream also became invisible as it clung to the door under all the layers of paint. There it survived until the dreamer was ready to value its hidden treasures and potential. Then it was uncovered.

The friends to whom I give the gifts in its pockets are some of the friends to whom I was introducing their dreams at this time. Women wore smocks during pregnancy. Pregnancy can be described as potential new life waiting to be brought to birth.

I asked myself what potential in me was covered over and protected but not brought to birth until now. Gold is a precious substance that does not tarnish with time. There is a process of refining whereby gold goes through many stages and must be tested in the furnace before it gets its stamp of quality. I too had been through many stages of process, had been tested and refined before I became able to give clear expression to my hidden, inner 'nuggets' of wisdom.

The knitted dolls and baby clothes suggest someone has been preparing and caring for this child, or potentiality, in me. The gifts or 'presents' - which sounds so much like 'presence' - were painted over but preserved, to be rediscovered at a later stage. During the time I dreamed this dream, I was beginning to discover aspects of myself previously unknown to me and as yet undeveloped.

It seemed significant that there were two knitted dolls, two packages - the gold locket suggesting space for two, one on each side. The symbol of a locket is about remembering, a place to store a picture of someone who should not be forgotten. The two knitted dolls lead me to Psalm 139:13 where it states, "It was you who created my inmost self, and put me together in my mother's womb." I marvel at the insight a dream can bring, even to evoke the word 'together' from that verse!

I often imagined as a child that I had a twin self with whom I could commune telepathically. I imagined no words were necessary for this communication. The sense that there was another me or aspect of me somewhere has kept me looking for that 'other part' for most of my life.

In recent times, much research has been undertaken in the field of embryology. Althea Hayton, in *Untwinned: Perspectives on the Death of a Twin before Birth,* says that, as far as can be ascertained from her vast research, up to 10% of the world's population are womb twin survivors of a twin or multiple pregnancy. It is possible that the dream was drawing my attention to this matter - long before the new information and research had reached me. This is also referenced and expanded upon by Jim Cogley in *The Twinless Self (Vol 4, Wood You Believe* series.)

Whether the quest was for another soul who may have begun life's journey with me, or for a hidden aspect of myself, might not matter in this particular dream. Perhaps, as so often, it was both. The gift or insight the dream brought me was the vivid experience that 'now I found what I was looking for.' I am no longer missing anything. I found a gold ring, symbol for wholeness. This is the crucial element in the dream.

I notice that the ring is 'where it belongs,' on the finger of the girl from the portrait who once lived in the house and wore this ring. This is symbolic of the part of me that once was whole. A ring also symbolises commitment and I am excited to rediscover my commitment to wholeness from such an early stage in my life.

Our earlier experiences often shape us and prepare us for the work of our soul's purpose in later life. It is the oyster that was wounded at an earlier stage that later produces the pearl. I came to understand from this dream that in this other realm called 'unconscious,' all was not lost, only preserved, until I was able to value it. Caring parents and teachers often protect children in a similar way from certain truths in life until they are emotionally mature enough to integrate or make sense of such things. Our unconscious, similar to a good parent, holds and protects that which ego is not yet mature enough to deal with or integrate.

Very sensitive children that were not protected or looked out for can often become caretakers in adult life. Their deprivations and painful experiences can yield inner wisdom, if carefully developed. This frees them to offer the care to others (those who mirror their own vulnerabilities) that they themselves were deprived of. Of course this does not absolve them of the responsibility to heal their own original wounds.

Amazing Grace

Whilst most of us are familiar with the hymn *Amazing Grace*, few are aware of its provenance. There was once an English sea captain called John Newton, operating a slaving ship plying the coasts of Africa and the British colonies. While involved in these crimes against humanity, Captain Newton had an extraordinary dream, transcribed below.

Inspired by dream wisdom, Newton utterly re-orientated his life and worked tirelessly with Mr William Wilberforce, MP, for the abolition of slavery.

Dream: Ring of Truth

In Derry, a stranger gives John Newton a ring, symbol of God and of perfection, as it has no beginning and no end. (It is also a well-known symbol of commitment and all that is ideal.) With this ring, Newton feels secure and happy in himself. Another man ridicules him and John throws the ring into the ocean, symbol of the unconscious.

The scene then changes to the Alps, where a fire is raging, which threatens to consume and destroy. Another man retrieves the ring, guards it and says, "I will guard it for you, and when you are ready or need it I will have it for you." The ring is now out of Newton's control, and he must submit to the situation.

Reflection: The opening scene features a stranger. Strangers in our dreams are as yet unknown aspects of our selves. Newton is given a gift, which he later discovers to be his salvation. The ridiculing character gives us a glimpse of the conflict within Newton's Psyche, causing him to push the troublesome feelings into the unconscious (the ring into the ocean). However, much as we like to think we have rid ourselves of such feelings, we are often faced each night with the very same elements we have failed to integrate or deal with in waking life. The retriever of the ring, by contrast, represents a wiser part of Newton's Self, possessed of an ability to guard this gift until the sailor, so far off course morally, is more able to develop it.

The notion of guardianship is interesting. Our potential for wholeness is often not lost, but 'contained' in our unconscious, waiting or being guarded, until we come into a fuller relationship with our Soul/Self and those chosen to cross our path on the journey bringing the Self to birth or wholeness or to consciousness. In this story, the message could not be clearer. Newton must retrieve the gift that was once given to him, the gift of living in truth that made him feel secure and happy in himself.

There is also an interesting change of scene. Fire is the energy of change. Nothing is ever the same after fire. What is left is different to what was before. When we think of raging fire in the mountains it suggests volcanic or major eruption, associated with anger and passion pouring out of us. Mountains, one easily observes, are symbolic of obstacles or challenges in life, and there was a need (conducted to great effect by the heroic Wilberforce) for an outpouring of anger at the systematic inhumanity being visited upon our fellow human beings. When we combine passion with righteous anger, it is amazing the changes that can be brought about.

William Wilberforce was on his deathbed when he received confirmation from Parliament that his bill to abolish slavery had just been passed.

Moved by this experience, John Newton then wrote *Amazing Grace*, "I once was lost but now am found, was blind but now I see…"

Dream: The Bones Are Numbered

In this dream there is a new house being built on the site of an unconsecrated and unmarked children's burial ground. The nuns are gathering up the bones in order to give them a proper burial or resting place. I notice that the bones are not all of babies and I am surprised to discover some are still not decomposed. One face looks like it had some distortion and still has flesh on it.

The nuns were doing this work with their bare hands and I went up to look. They were using paper cards with markings and numbers of identification. I asked my brother if he might know who was building the new house. He did not know his name, only that he was new to this area.

Reflection: To understand the important context of this dream, it is necessary to explain why these babies were buried in such a manner, without ceremony. Such graveyards were known as *Lisheens* and are to be found in most Irish communities. Babies who died at or shortly after birth and who had not received the Sacrament of Baptism were believed to be without grace and therefore deemed unfit for burial in consecrated ground.

I had this dream in 1996. At this time the Church was beginning to revise its thinking on *Lisheens* and was offering to say Mass for the souls of those infants. Today we have special altars built in some graveyards to remember these souls. They are known in Irish as *Altóir na bPáistí* (Children's Altar) and they are also remembered in registers kept alongside the Baptism registers.

The dream shows that a new development is about to happen. A new house is about to be built, but first, that which was buried without proper respect must be dug up and identified before being laid to rest in a more appropriate manner. Rituals, such as proper acknowledgement and blessing of the dead, are a vital part of our outer life.

The dream offers us a clear image of an inner ritual that takes place in our Psyche each night. The fact that the bones are being numbered and identified must be underlined. Our dreams offer us the opportunity to identify aspects of ourselves that we have buried. They help us to deal with unresolved emotions or beliefs in order to make progress with new development. We lay old hurts to rest in peace, instead of allowing them to be buried alive in shame and ignorance.

The nuns in the dream were 'numbering the bones.' This echoes Psalm 22, which foreshadows the Crucifixion. It begins with the line, "My God my God, why have you deserted me?" then, in verses 17 and 18 it reads, "I can count every one of my bones… They divide my garments among them and cast lots for my clothes."

You could say the souls of all those innocent souls felt forsaken too and finally were accounted for!

The man who is going to build the new house, or symbol of Animus (male side of the feminine Psyche) in the dream, is 'new' in my area. This could represent the new thinking in Church behaviour. And it could represent a new development in my own life. I think it does both. (The word 'Animus' will be dealt with and developed under 'Archetypes' in later chapters.)

Chapter Three

Developing Awareness

The earth is heavy and opaque without dreams.
Anaïs Nin, *The Diary of Anaïs Nin, Vol.3*

The critical point is the decision to be attentive, or not, to the gifts of our unconscious. On this commitment hinges more than might be thought! The decisions of those who deliberately chose the way of attentiveness affected, not only lives, but also, nations and epochs.

The signs are good that you are voting for dream-wisdom, since you have read this far into the book! There are other ways to signal to your unconscious that you are in reception mode, ready to receive transmissions from, what fax machines would call, a 'distant station.'

Dream Journals

The single most substantial move you can make to indicate your seriousness about paying this sort of attention is to buy a notebook dedicated to that purpose.

Think of the dreaming Self as a Gifts-bearer, a guest invited to our home. By offering the intention to be attentive when we awake (both to the experience of those moments and the dream-memories themselves) we are sending out an invitation to the Dreamer-Self. And, as in life, when we are hosts, it then becomes our happy duty to show up when our guests arrive. It is no good inviting guests, in real life or otherwise, if you aren't planning to be there to welcome them. When it comes to your invited Dreamer-Self, the way to welcome them or show up is by greeting them before going to encounter the other customary companions of each dawning day, like your clock or your bathroom mirror or your breakfast show DJ.

Be there, pen in hand, and jot down the notes.

Buy a notebook, a set of index cards and a smooth-flowing pen. Leave them at the ready on your bedside table. The index cards should be left to hand to jot down the dream in that 'in-between' state on waking, even before you pull away the duvet and your feet touch the floor. These notes can then be the basis for the properly detailed dream transcript in your journal later in the day. Or you might prefer to use the back of the journal for these jottings and then the front of the journal for the written-out narratives. Your journal should not be any old school jotter, flimsily bound and designed for disposability. Remember that each dream is a gift and thus deserves to be enclosed between lasting covers, preferably in a binding that is satisfying to hold and on paper pleasant to write upon.

Gene recorded and painted the following dream in her journal during her therapy process.

Dream: Embroidery

I am in a therapy session where I talk and Kathleen listens. At the end of the session, Kathleen hands me four pages of paper from my journal. The outer two pages serve as a cover for the inner two. The inner pages are covered in beautifully embroidered flowers, pink and white, like flowering cherry blossoms. The flowers also look like butterflies at rest, with their pink-and-white wings folded up and at ease. I wondered why one of these pages was right way up and the opposite one was upside down. The petals or butterfly wings were delicately and meticulously embroidered.

I also noticed how easy it would have been for the piercing needlework to have torn the paper and thought to myself how the paper could not have bent as easily as it was quite brittle and prone to tearing. This work took extortionate care and patience. I wondered why Kathleen had chosen to embroider on such delicate paper and not on cloth.

Reflection: This brief dream reflects the nature of our work together. Gene sees me as the one doing the 'delicate' needlework. To 'needle' someone could be seen as a way of getting to the sensitive point of a matter. Her Dream-Self shows me handing material back to her, the pages from her own journal. This was indeed what happened in our process. Each week Gene would bring in material from her journal, in which she was recording her dreams as well as other material she was working through by journaling. Although the paper was fragile, we see it was possible to work with it without damaging or tearing it. This was to represent the delicate yet durable quality of our therapeutic relationship. The work was well described in the image of delicate and intricate embroidery offered by the dream, and required, as her dream stated, 'extortionate' care and patience in paying due attention to detail.

The four pages could also represent the foreword to the work. The outer two pages formed a cover to protect the delicate inner pages, containing the exquisite work. When our world is turned upside down, we have a chance to see things from a completely different perspective, as was indeed the case when Gene's world was looked at through the prism of dreams. In giving back to Gene the material she had already brought in, the dream shows the transforming quality of the work. This was represented beautifully by the butterfly resting on the cherry blossom. Metaphorically, Gene was in the process of spreading her own wings. Each session became a resting place to reflect on all that was being transformed within her as she was coming to blossom in her own life. Dreams are often described as 'fleeting,' as indeed are cherry blossoms. Each makes a profound statement and calls attention to their magnificence.

Gene also shared her own reflection with me. "Upon exploring the dream with Kathleen in the conscious world of wakefulness, I was to discover my self as the embroiderer. We discovered that I was the paper, and the embroidery was my journaling of my process. All the meticulous attention to detail and the patience required in taking this journey is depicted in the artwork. The end result is a beautiful piece of art, pink and delicate, to represent my feminine side. I had noticed earlier this spring how the cherry blossom trees had blossomed earlier than usual. I feel very positive about the suggestion of my own, earlier than expected, 'blossoming' in my search for meaning from my dreams."

Between the Worlds

That place between the two worlds, the fully asleep and the fully awake, is a special place, and you need to dwell there as long as you can to tune in to the dream wisdom. In Irish we use the term, *idir eatharthu,* between worlds. Whether we are a child or a financier, a dictator or a poet, all humans pass through that place. Some might try to get out of it as fast as possible, but not us.

Never has art more perfectly captured the sensation of being between these worlds than in Fellini's remarkable *Roma*. You may remember a sequence close to the ending of that film when workers, excavating underground, come across a lost Roman palace, decorated with sumptuous frescoes showing aristocrats and dancers, gentlewomen and slaves in every shade of robe, and some without. The workers move gingerly into the decorated cavities, unseen for at least a millennium and a half. In wonder, they run their torches over the exquisitely painted expanses as the air of contemporary Rome whistles in over their heads through the small entrance hole they just created. And then disaster strikes. That very air begins to destroy the frescoes, peeling them away in minutes until all that remains is bare wall.

Just so, do we wake, finding ourselves in a hidden palace filled with the most vivid of images. And just so, does the air of the incoming day wipe away almost all the traces of that mysterious artistry, the images of a lost world.

Just so, unless we are prepared! We must, as far as possible, be ready to stop up the hole through which come the sights and sounds of the incoming day: breakfast radio banter, peace-shattering digital alarms, strategic thoughts of the day ahead. Take steps to **make your awakening more gradual** and less stressful. Perhaps you could even wake a little earlier than is strictly necessary to allow time for lingering in this place so full of image-gifts. You might even find that silence is more conducive to gradual waking than shrill, high frequency pips. Some people might assume that the less bracing sounds of a classical music station might be appropriate. I advise against it, however relaxing the sounds of Mozart and Haydn can be, they are still foreign to your dream-world and remove you from that place, however gently.

Muse and Wander

Besides these practical steps, buying a dedicated notebook and changing our waking patterns, we must cultivate a particular disposition towards the gifts of our unconscious. A novelist once advised beginning writers to open up a 'warm expectancy' within themselves as they develop their storytelling ideas. So it should be with your dream-work. Like a shopkeeper expecting a fresh assortment of goods from the warehouse, **be open for the 'business' of the soul**.

In the first chapter of this book, we learned that dreams matter to all of us but that our interpretations can be impaired, sometimes because of our loyalty to authorities. And sometimes our access to dream-wisdom can be restricted because we are alienated from our unconscious selves one way or another, often by everyday distractions but also out of sheer 'symbol-blindness.' We resist seeing the meaning of things, even when they are patent. Our undertaking in this book is to look afresh at the language of dreams, to be open and attentive to the symbols, images and (frequently unusual) elements they contain.

Taking Dreams Seriously

All sorts of things can happen when we take our dreams seriously. In recent decades, with the boom in self-expression, we are encouraged to 'follow our dreams.' Do not only follow dreams in the sense of *aspirations*. Great achievers from Vivaldi to Steve Jobs would be unheard of today if they had not taken their 'dreams,' in that aspirational sense, with a seriousness that called for a life's devotion. We are all familiar with the call to take practical steps to realise what one might call our 'achievement-fantasies.' These dreams are the healthy and productive visions of how we might best become ourselves. But, in this book, we are calling for you to **take your actual dreams seriously**, the *night-visions* playing out in the cinema of your mind whenever sleep comes. Remarkable things can happen when those visions are attended to.

Ireland's patron saint, the great Saint Patrick, is a perfect example. He was a lifelong recipient of dream-messages. Had he not been, we might never have heard of him, and the history of Ireland would have been changed irrevocably.

If you remember his story, Patrick's early life was marred by kidnapping. He was stolen from his home as a boy and brought to Ireland and to the harsh state of slavery. For six years, he toiled as a shepherd until, one night, a voice came to him in a dream telling of a ship awaiting his boarding. That passage to freedom, the Saint tells us in his *Confessions,* turned out to be two hundred miles away. Imagine hearkening to such a far-fetched message! And yet, the young Patrick found the courage to heed his dreams with the gravity they deserved. It was time for him to move on and take control of his destiny.

Patrick studied and became a priest and bishop, all the while taking pains to understand correctly the often strange messages placed before his conscious mind. Then came the most momentous of his 'visions of the night,' a call from the Irish, his former persecutors, to "come and walk again amongst us." Patrick recalls himself as "stung intensely in my heart" in this dream, a valuable example to us to never neglect recording how we *feel* in the dream.

Sometimes we can be so focused on recording the particulars, we can neglect to set down the emotions we experienced in the dream-state.

In both the dreams, Patrick cleaves hard to the promptings of a spiritual self, and in tandem with prayer and deed, materialises his visions as conscious reality. By taking up invitations to wisdom from our dreams, we too can shake free of slavish behaviour. Indeed, our Psyche is a tireless secretary, forever on duty and taking 'inner notes' about the state of our Soul on its journey towards purpose, and will continue to find ways (especially when the Ego is off-duty!) to get through to us. **"Dreams," as Marsha Norman puts it, "are illustrations... from the book your soul is writing about you."**

The question has already been asked whether history makes human beings or whether human beings make history! Whichever is the truth, it is important to recall and record the facts of history. Similarly, when working with a dream, we must look carefully at where the dream finds the images used. The Dream-Self knows us intimately and naturally has access to all that we have experienced. With the greatest efficiency, the Dream-Self uses whatever is most effective to achieve intimate contact with us.

Ideally, we continue to learn and grow from past mistakes. These errors are often rooted in fear and result in the need to control and suppress. This is caused by an undeveloped sense of responsibility.

In the same way that our public history is recorded and not always made public until many years later, when it may take a tribunal to elicit the full facts, you could say that our 'inner team' of dream characters are busy taking notes of the actual facts of our lives and that these facts are to be presented later (in the form of a dream) when the ego least expects to be confronted.

We are constantly gathering information as we go about our daily lives, and almost unknown to our conscious mind, this 'input feed' is constantly seeping into our Psyche. From this vast storehouse of collected images and stimuli, the Creative Editor within fashions mini-documentaries about our way of being in the world, and in the body.

Sometimes we wake up from a busy dream, seeming real, until the second our conscious mind takes over. In that instant, all can feel wiped out and lost, as this next dream shows.

Dream: Time to Take a Stand

I am typing some interesting content for my book, about the significance of the need to take a stand, and do something with the accumulated relevant information gathered. I see lots of newspapers and some cuttings from papers, and I am making connections between the content of the newspapers and the content of the unconscious, both containing all sorts of information and detail about every aspect of life. In the dream, I am consciously typing the detail on my laptop and I know it is for my book.

Reflection: As I woke up, I realised that I was dreaming and it felt as if all my (dream) effort of typing was lost, just as we feel when accidentally deleting a significant piece of work. But, when all seems lost, we must hover in that in-between place for the next couple of minutes if we are to recapture the essence of the dream wisdom.

It was 6:30am. As I tried to save the memory of the dream, I scanned my recent activities for any newspaper headlines that might have caught my attention and recalled a story about the conflict between China and the Dalai Lama. At the time, the Olympic Games were coming to China, presenting an ideal opportunity to draw the world's attention to China's illegal occupation of Tibet and its persecution of her exiled spiritual leader, the Dalai Lama. In the newspaper article, he called for an end to violence and asked the world to remember the decades of repression that Tibetans endured under China's rule. I had also taken note some months before of Stephen Spielberg's withdrawal from the Games' ceremonies to draw attention to Tibet's struggle.

I could not help but see the archetypal parallels and see them still today many years later. China, with all its power and concern for image on the world stage, represents the Ego, and Tibet, denied its original spirituality and individual freedom, represents a Self that is refusing to be denied any longer. Just as in the outer world of conflict and punishments, there are consequences for the uprising of the Self. Such a revolt can feel like death to the Ego, as long as it is trying to resist and control instead of respect and work with the Self. The time has come for the world to be made aware of the Tibetan situation as it really is. In the eyes of the world, be it the wider world or the world of our own individual lives, we all know how important it is to be seen to 'look good.'

Just as the world has the potential to be whole and wholly holy, and at one with its many continents, countries, states and its peoples, we must start with the same possibility, that as individuals, we too must come into wholeness and holiness with the many diverse aspects of ourselves.

Through our dreams, we are invited and encouraged to liberate the aspects of our own Psyche, which, at ego level, we continue to dominate and suppress. Image is always in danger of being tarnished when facts are exposed. The image of being well-off financially can be projected by the overuse of plastic cards and by overdrawing our bank accounts. Ego, similarly, can survive as long as it represses the reality of the 'bank account.' However, when the bank statement comes, we are presented with the facts. Our dream statements have the very same function.

Remember the previous dream. Our dreams can be likened to daily newspapers, reporting the doings of all and sundry from our inner world. And, just as in newspapers, some topics are more memorable than others and seem to make memorable headlines in big print as we wake up. The challenge, on an individual level, is no less than that on the global level, i.e. what do we do with this information? Do we ignore it and say it does not affect us, or do we take the time to take note and responsibility for information and wisdom that is available to us?

The Ego becomes bruised or cracked as the Self emerges. In a similar way, bullies lose power as victims find their voice. It might seem unlikely to the perpetrator of some crime or act of violence, who has power over a timid or frightened child, that one day this same timid child will grow up sufficiently to speak out. When this happens, the facts are exposed and the balance of power begins to shift, and the wounded Self (or child or country) can begin to recover and heal.

Other Cultures, Other Ways

We do well to remember that just because things are done in a particular way in our time and our place, it does not mean things necessarily have to be so. Modern Western culture, with its emphasis on development of the rational and scientific mind, conditions us to over-identify with 'objective' events and circumstances while downplaying the 'subjective.' In our consumption-orientated drive towards wealth and security, we have neglected a rich inner resource, a language of myth and symbol that seems to survive only in folklore and legend. And, in giving up our religious rituals, we are left hungering for the sustenance they originally provided.

Elsewhere and in other times, people organised themselves quite differently and benefitted from the results. One of the pioneer psychologists already mentioned, Marie-Louise Von Franz, noted that the native peoples of Canada relied on dreams and visions during difficult times. Their prophets, for example, foresaw through dream-wisdom the disastrous consequences of the White Man's arrival. The Unconscious tried to furnish a way to adapt, but, tragically in this instance, the Conscious was unable to cope with, or understand the message on the proper psychological level.

Our dreams may be the only Theatres of Ritual left to us and if society will not buy a ticket, you certainly can. **Form your own dream-derived ritual**, start by recording the dreams and taking their counsel.

The Source of Dream Wisdom

Be aware of why we take the time to tune in to our dreams. The clearest statement of what they offer would run as follows:

When we listen to our dreams and work with their wisdom, we take guidance from our Soul. The function of the dream is to draw attention to (or bring into consciousness) unconscious aspects of Self. The dream strives to protect and guide the dreamer but the conscious mind finds it challenging to embrace and integrate the unconscious content. So we need to develop awareness, by being prepared to attend to our dreams.

That, in a nutshell, is what the first part of our journey together in this book is about. History has many examples of men and women who have found superior intelligence and life guidance from their unconscious. But where does this wisdom come from? And how can we become best acquainted with its source?

My own first inkling of these matters came in the 1980s, when I was travelling in the United States. Many readers will relate to the experience I describe, since dreams are often a portal into what our rational minds tell us to be 'impossible.'

Dream: At the Funeral

I am walking with a close friend, Edwina, behind a coffin surrounded by many young people. The funeral is in my hometown.

Reflection: On returning to Ireland a week later, I discovered that Edwina really *did* have to walk behind a coffin while I was away and had missed my supportive presence. Her boyfriend, Darren, died in an accident in Scotland on the same day *and at the same time* as I had my dream in Florida. Alongside my immense sadness and loss, I marvelled at this dream. How had the information of this unexpected death reached me? Who (or what source of intelligence) was responsible?

This experience was followed by more prophetic and synchronistic dreams, i.e. the contemporaneous coming together of disparate outer and inner events, in ways we often dismiss as coincidental. Naturally, I wanted to get to know more about the source of this knowledge and learn how to relate to these messages, cloaked though they were in the language of symbol and image. That dream, if any, started me on my journey. If there was a dreamer within sending me these messages, I wanted to know her.

Exercise: Taking Note

Buy a notebook and some index cards. On the index cards jot down whatever you can remember in that intermediate state, described previously, between being fully asleep and fully awake. Later in the day, make time to write up these jottings into a dated dream transcript in your journal.

Chapter Four

Further Guidance

Sleep is the God and master of our senses.
Lope de Vega

In Chapter Two we read a series of dreams about dreaming, calls from the Psyche that messages are forthcoming and should be hearkened to. Now, we examine a quartet of dreams that embody the quintessence of dream wisdom. The particular nuggets of wisdom extracted from the dreams below were based on a knowledge of who I was, how I tended to respond or react, and where these traits came from. Beyond that, my dreams revealed how I might bring about change by exploring my feelings and emotions. Your dream wisdom is the very same. Within your dream life is an **individually grounded appeal to action, growth and change**. But it is not the kind of generic appeal we are familiar with from advertising or standard issue self-help literature. These appeals are grounded in an intimate understanding of who we are, and why we are the way we are and how we might best go forward.

This guidance from the Soul both challenges and encourages us to develop our instinctual nature, as we find in the opening 'movement' of our quartet.

Dream: *Follow Your Nose*

I'm in a theatre. I seem to have entered from some side door, and I am up front. The place is fairly empty and this surprises me. The act on stage is to follow your nose. People on stage get up and move around the stage following their noses! A woman comes in, and she acknowledges me. She has a very creative nose made and is displaying it as she follows it around the stage as a demonstration. The noses are made like masks.

Reflection: This short dream makes a clear statement. Remember in Chapter One how we established the importance of noticing the setting of the opening scene? Here is a perfect example of a setting giving a revealing context to the rest of the action. In this dream, we find that the location is a theatre, a place where we get to sit back and see the drama of life unfold. Note also that even though I seem to have come in by some side door, I am up front. Pay attention to the message! 'Up front' is another way of saying 'being honest or straight.' And it is no accident that I have come in through a side door. Entering through a side or back door suggests a sense of familiarity, whereas going through the front door is more formal.

The fact that there are not many people in the theatre could suggest that not many people are interested in this play or way of being in the world. Perhaps the material being presented is too challenging? Remember that we have been shaped to develop logic more than intuition or instinct. Any performance featuring the 'non-logical' is unlikely to appeal to a wide audience.

The woman in the dream, a symbol of the Feminine Principle, acknowledges my presence and seems to know me. Although the visual image is dramatic and creative (she demonstrates how to follow one's nose), **the message is revealed in the metaphor** and that message, making explicit what is implicit, could not be more simple and direct.

And what a delightful sense of humour is invoked in the dramatisation of that metaphor!

I welcomed this dream as an invitation to trust and follow my own instinct. What did this mean in real life? I would have to give up my regular job (with a secure income) and risk setting up a practice in psychotherapy. This had to be done in a region where such an undertaking was unprecedented. I needed a place from which to work. Telling my bank manager that I was going to 'follow my nose' regarding mortgage payments seemed a stretch when I was also buying a house at this time! But where would we be if we left all our decision-making in the hands of bank managers or our own 'internal bank manager,' the Ego? Only with the input of the different parts of ourselves, Masculine and Feminine, Ego and Unconscious, can we make the fully informed and meaningful decisions that make for a fulfilling life.

The House of the Self

Carl G. Jung describes the **house as the Self,** and just as a house needs constant upkeep and sometimes restoration work, so does the Self. The following dream puts me in touch with my Self as I explore this most interesting house.

Dream: House as Symbol of Self

I am looking at an old house which is for sale and am fascinated by its potential. The auctioneer puts on a light, as it seems dark with only one window visible.

At first it looks as if it has only one main room and one bedroom, but he shows me a partition that leads to a huge, high room behind the wall. It looks as if a cupboard conceals the door in the partition. This newly discovered room has a very high ceiling and lots of space and many interesting things in it that I would love to browse through - children's things, all sorts.

I seem to be showing all this to a female psychotherapy client and am still excited about its content and potential. I show her behind the partition, and again, I see what could be done with this space. I am aware that I have already looked at this for myself in the past, but now that I have my own house, which doesn't seem nearly as interesting, I feel some sense of loss of opportunity. I notice there are no light bulbs, but somehow I find light. The woman tells me she needs a place to rest in, and this could be such a cosy place. It has one large dresser and a couple of comfortable couches.

We are now on our way out when I realise I haven't yet shown her the bottom room inside the door. We have noticed that there is a pot of something boiling on an old-fashioned fireplace. We are outside, and even though the others are here, I bring her in to show her the other room. Someone is sleeping there, and as we enter he slips out. He is someone I seem to recognise. For some reason it bothers me but I don't embarrass him by acknowledging it. It's obvious there is a woman in bed with him.

Now, there is panic as the others come, only to discover they are all my family members. We are all talking, and I'm remembering I had taken my father to see this place before. A nice young man helps my father up and shows him around while I'm busy discovering things. Suddenly there is a bit of panic as a child wakes up and is crying. The child is on a straw-covered floor on a high loft-like level. The man who had been asleep earlier comes in with a stretcher covered in straw, and he is also wearing a jacket made of straw. The woman has the child covered in straw. He takes mother and child outside. My sister looks at me and makes some comment about their condition but no one makes any judgment about the fact that they seem to have been squatting.

I then discover a little cabinet hanging on the wall, and it is full of jewellery. I am tempted to take it but don't. My cousin comes and tells us it is time to go. I am reluctant to leave and ask her where they are going. I have something in my pocket, not from the jewellery cabinet but from the children's things.

The man has lifted my father up onto the higher level. The place has so much potential and lots of work to be done, and yet, it could be lovely as it is and most interesting. I am again aware that I have been here before and wonder if the price had been too high at that earlier time.

Reflection: Here is a house sorely in need of discovery and investment (remember the identification of Self and House that Jung alerted us to.) I am looking to invest in this 'House' or Self (by establishing my professional practice) and as I show the premises to my client I realise that I must continue to provide myself what I am offering my client, a place to rest and discover inner treasures, treasures that have been shelved or hidden away. Yes, that is a challenge, but to do otherwise would be to ignore all aspects of the dream as aspects of Self.

It is interesting to note that as the child (representing new potential) wakes up, the floor and bed are covered in straw. There is something of the nature of the Nativity Crib in this scene. I remember my grandmother recalling the birth of her children on a bed of straw on the floor of her home.

Marion Woodman, in *The Pregnant Virgin*, refers to the child who appears in a dream in straw, bulrushes or a barn as symbolic of the Divine Child - radiant with light, robust, intelligent and sensitive.

Let's consider what else is in this house. Looking behind the partition is like peering behind our own division and discovering elements there in an original, 'unimproved' state. And the fact that something is boiling on the old fireplace suggests that there is nourishment here or at least potential to make tea.

Browsing through the children's things could be about browsing through my own childhood, as I was doing in waking reality with this particular client. If I were to make conscious what I might have taken secretly (in my pocket) from my childhood, I think it would be my desire for justice, or in my child's mind, a sense of fairness, holiness (or wholeness) and belonging.

Looking back on this dream I wonder if we are indeed all but squatters on this Earth and in need of awakening to reality at higher levels. Note also the reference to having been here before, which could allude to reincarnation. This was to be the year my father was raised to that higher level, as he passed away before the year was out.

Dream: Divine Energies at Work on my House.

In this dream I notice that the entire Devine family, as I know them, are working on building my house. The scene is from my childhood ideal site. I notice that various members of this family are working on all levels of my new house. Some work inside while others work on the outside. The significant thing is that the Father figure is working at the highest level on the roof. I feel very excited.

Reflection: At this time, I was excited in my discoveries of the house being the symbol of Self from my reading of Carl Jung. I was excited to note the pun on the family name my dream chose to deliver the message. The human Devine family became a symbol for me in several other dreams to indicate the Divine message.

The fact that this dream is located on the site of my childhood idealism seems to suggest that my deepest desire was already heard by my Divine family of origin. It was as if the Father figure was overseeing all the work being done and involved himself at the highest level.

Integrating New and Old

One year later, the following dream arrived:

Dream: Higher Level Work and Development

At the end of our road and in a field that I had known as wasteland, a man, whose name is the same as my old teacher's, though it is not he, has built a magnificent building. The old house is completely transformed and incorporated into the new structure. There's also a village of other new houses there. Everyone seems to be amazed at the magnificence of this building. I go inside to have a look, and as I enter from a side or back door, I too find myself amazed at what it's like.

I look up to the ceiling where there is the head of a man coming through a hole in the ceiling where he is working on it. I am in awe at the way he works as I watch him and especially at the way he blends colours into each other. The way he works from this position is most unusual. It looks like the Master Artist is at work (just like the work of Michelangelo on the ceiling of the Sistine Chapel).

I ask him if I can look around. He says "Yes" as long as I am in my bare feet (no shoes are allowed). I notice the fireplace is in cast iron and the attention to detail is exquisite. Lucy comes in and I am excited to see her. It's as if this place used to be hers. It was called 'St. Francis.'

Reflection: This dream seems to acknowledge work done or in the process of development. To get at the essence of the dream (always our goal – dream wisdom is in the essential) I used a therapeutic method known as **Gestalt**.

Gestalt psychology is a theory of perception which was developed by Fritz Perls, a German originally trained in Freudian psychoanalysis and later influenced by Existentialism. His breakthrough encouraged individuals to give a 'here-and-now' voice to the characters and symbols in our dreams, thus encouraging the dreamer to own each element and acknowledge its root in the Self. If you have been in therapy, you may be familiar with the technique. Perhaps your therapist asked you a question like this: "If the silent visitor in your dream could speak, what would they say?"

In interpreting the dream I asked myself to spontaneously give the magnificent building a voice. What would it say?

"I am where you'd have least expected to find me."

What would the workman say?

"While you thought I was wasting my potential, I have in fact been developing and working on this structure. And yes, it is different. *I'm* different. I have incorporated the old house into this much developed newer one."

Why did I need to take my shoes off?

"Because I do not want outside stuff coming in on shoes and it is to respect this work and this place."

In response, I tell him he looks like the Face of God as I imagine Him painted by the great artists on the church ceilings.

The dream suggests inner sacred work and transformation. I am pleased to note that the old structure was not demolished but incorporated into something new. As children, we used to call our teacher 'the Master' and in this dream I was happy to see, because of the Dream Master's far more creative manner, I had a different teacher to learn from than the one I was given as a child.

Traditionally the fireplace, (another key symbol), is a place of warmth or sharing and of gathering. Unfortunately, this was not my experience of our fireplace in our schoolroom where the teacher was the one to benefit most from its heat. My dream, in keeping with my experience as a student therapist with a much more creative 'Master,' was certainly expressing the possibility of another way.

Serviam

The other (and perhaps most challenging) aspect of this dream might be the message delivered, as commercial advertisements do on the television, in the last line. The closing of a dream is of special interest, as stated in the principles of Chapter One.

The fact that Lucy enters the dream house is not what seems to matter, but my *association* with Lucy, who, in real life, worked in a place called 'St. Francis.' After some puzzlement, I realised that Francis of Assisi was a pivotal figure in my quest for vocational meaning.

The first gift I received for my workroom was the prayer of St Francis:

"Lord, make me an instrument of your peace. Where there is hatred let me sow love. Where there is injury, pardon. Where there is doubt, faith. Where there is despair, hope. Where there is darkness, light. Where there is sadness, joy. O Divine Master, grant that I may not so much seek to be consoled as to console. To be understood as to understand. To be loved as to love. For it is in giving that we receive. It is in pardoning that we are pardoned. It is in dying that we are born to eternal life."

In the Franciscan ethos lay the answer to my questions, becoming an instrument, *serving*. When I qualified as a psychotherapist I was at first unsure about where I might find work and how I would develop my professional confidence. Then I remembered the teaching from the Bible: "Then he said to his disciples, 'The harvest is rich but the labourers are few, so ask the Lord of the harvest to send labourers to his harvest.'" (Matthew 9:37)

I did just this and through my prayer I said, "Lord I am ready to be put to work." It was in this spirit that I decided to take a one-year leave of absence from work to gain experience as a therapist. At this time I had the next dream.

Dream: Honey

I have put a jar of honey bearing my brand name into a health food store for trial. I get a phone call from the owner, telling me she wants more jars of my honey to meet the demand. I resist at first as I have not anticipated such demand but she insists that I must keep up the supply.

Reflection: Isn't honey a rich metaphor? In fact, there are few natural substances that are as rich and none as sweet. But, beyond taste, honey possesses healing properties and is a thoroughly natural gift from the bees. We often take these productive insects for granted and remain mostly unappreciative of their highly evolved system. But, without their role in the pollination cycle, the human species might well not exist.

Following Gestalt techniques, I gave the honey a voice: "I have natural healing properties, and there is a huge demand for me in the marketplace." This has continued to be my experience since that day. As Seth Godin puts it, "the number one way to attract people is to help them connect with their dreams." That is my role in the spiritual 'pollination cycle' that keeps us growing as adults, making connections between the wisdom gifted us by our Unconscious and the deliberations of the Conscious mind.

Moreover, just like the busy bee, little of the work that goes on behind the scenes is visible to spectators. But untasted honey may as well taste of treacle. It was time for me to bring the healing honey of my work to the marketplace.

Expressing the Details

We have seen in the dreams above that the smallest of details (the contents of a pocket, for example, or a boiling kettle) can be precious for our purposes. Detail presents a real challenge for the seeker of dream wisdom. The attempt to do justice to the elaborate detail of some dreams reminds me of my experience of the great Spanish architect, Antoni Gaudí.

I remember standing before Gaudí's work in Barcelona and speculating on their origins. He must, I thought to myself, have first seen these buildings in his dreams. The fact that I could not even find the words in my mind to adequately describe his creativity was also a sign that their source lay deeper than consciousness. This man managed to build what most of us could only imagine in our dreams. There was another piece of persuasive evidence for my theory. Experiencing his legacy, I felt as if I were in the ocean, in that watery realm which we know to represent the unconscious. Indeed I was effectively passing into a dream state as I moved around his spaces, trying to absorb the detail.

Reading about Gaudí afterwards, I found myself in awe of his humility. This mystical and pious man could only have found such genius in the depths of his innermost being, that place where each one of us can draw on the great divine creative source. The critic Juan-Eduardo Cirlot described one of his well-known creations, the pavilions in *Parc Güell,* as "almost worshipful of childish myths and dreamlike atmosphere," expressing "faith in everything that was beautiful and divinely demonstrated." A later writer, the poet Wane Visser, on Gaudí's works stated, "They echo creation/And spark revelation."

That was certainly true of my contemplations in Barcelona.

How did Gaudí conceive the physical form for these remarkable images? Delving into his process, I learned that he profoundly respected the laws of nature and integrated the technically inclined and imaginative aspects of his Psyche. And, as dreamers do, he looked to his native place for inspiration, using local raw materials such as sandstone, glass and tile.

In the end, like some great dreams perhaps, one has to leave the world of Gaudí, not fully interpreted, as something to be experienced and perhaps changed by, as I was, forever after. Gaudí is a reminder that the realm of the marvellous can exist for us all and that the work to be done in reaching that level is ongoing. (His extraordinary Temple

De La Sagrada Familia is still being built...) Does this not remind you of the realm of dreams? They also leave us with a glimpse of the possible in our own lives and with our own abilities as the bricks-and-mortar. Dreams also leave us with work to be continued. To return to Wane Visser's poem, they stir us, "To be builder and breaker/ To become a dream-shaper."

Taking Guidance

There are practical ways in which, having resolved to be attentive, we extract the most essence out of the material being vouchsafed us as we sleep. Remember the dance of the bees - to get the most 'nectar' we need to be approaching the right flower from the right direction.

Make no mistake, the urgings from the Soul that we find in our dreams are not there to entertain or divert us. They offer guidance, but usually in a form we have to work with to incorporate into our decision-making. The dream wisdom we have seen in this chapter is the result of patient, ruminative divination, in tandem with techniques such as Gestalt. This approach yielded the essential messages I needed, fortifying and **guiding** me on my professional path to its conclusion, helping people to become more conscious.

You might argue that my conscious mind would have come to the right conclusion eventually, without any regard to my night visions. To which I would reply that I have listened to my dreams, and they have directed my life in a way that I couldn't have consciously imagined. And my life is by far the better for it.

Exercise: Voice of the Symbol

Select one of the more striking dream transcripts in your journal. Look at the symbols that have emerged. Perhaps there is an outsized radio in a corner, a teapot filled with daisies or a floating car. The ways of the sleeping mind are infinite! Once you have settled on a potent symbol and have time and space to think, give that element a voice. What would it say if it could talk? Take note, and respond.

Chapter Five

Learning the Language of Dreams

Night is the morning's canvas.
Emily Dickinson

And if you could hear
The whispering of the dream
You would hear no other sound.
Kahlil Gibran, *The Prophet*

Having acknowledged that the Soul is uniquely pleased to offer us the guidance we need, we must now look at the particular 'Language' of the Soul in order to benefit from Dream Wisdom. Every tongue has its own ways. For example, in Latin and German, the verbs can come at the end of the sentence. In the Irish language, there is no direct translation of the word, 'No.' If you are stepping outside your native language, as we are here, it is helpful to know some of the patterns and devices you are likely to encounter.

We will pause, as we go, to consider some valuable concepts that can help us better understand this new language. Think of them like those 'guides to the culture' you might find in the pages of a good foreign language primer.

Scene and Position

One pattern always worth noting is the **opening scene**. In a dream, this usually points us in the direction of the time or place in our lives from which the dream draws data to alert us to aspects in need of attention. Similarly, the stage setting for a play can tell us much about a production even before the characters appear. The atmosphere and content give us many clues and we need to be curious enough to register them. Each night we become 'theatre goers' presented with a 'production' from our Higher Self to our Conscious Self in an attempt to show us how we are doing on the journey we have chosen toward wholeness. And the 'Producer' is the most creative part of ourselves, with her own reason and wisdom in choosing and presenting detail.

Another aspect to observe is the **position** the dreamer finds themselves in. The following dream is an example.

In this dream, Agnes' Higher Self urges her towards healthier behaviour. From childhood, Agnes was poorly mothered. Her mother felt ill equipped for her role and instead of dealing with those fears, tried to control her daughter with anger and violence. In turn, Agnes is now married to a man she fears. Instead of dealing with her fears she tries to control him with anger and violence, repeating a pattern of behaviour that was destructive then and remains so now, not only to her children, but also her relationship.

Dream: Mother and Daughter

Agnes' mother is dying, slipping in and out of consciousness. Agnes tells her she loves her and is very upset. The doctor tells her it will only be a short time until her mother dies. She is being brought home along the old road to die there, while Agnes cycles her bike on a new road that is being built. On this new road, new houses are being developed and she is cycling towards the house of a woman called Anne. At this point she sees her husband banging his head on a glass wall and bleeding. She is not tempted to rescue him, but continues on her way to a place where her mother is about to die. Her mother sends her the text of a poem as she approaches. The family gather around her and sing as she dies. There is also a character from a TV soap opera present. The atmosphere is more of celebration than loss.

Reflection: At the time of her dream Agnes was working on changing the destructive aspect of her behaviour. The dream dramatises the coming 'death' of this old ill-health (the destructive behaviour itself) while the healing aspect of her Self (the doctor) reassures her that it is only a matter of time until she 'dies.'

It is essential to take note of the position the dreamer is in. In this dream, Agnes is going towards Anne's dwelling (Anne representing the healthy mother), when she chooses the new road. Her own mother is on the old road, on her way home to die. So Agnes is encouraged to believe that she is on a healthy path, the outcome of which is already within view, though she is not quite there yet.

We see also that it is important to bring her home. In other words, Agnes' behaviour needs to be 'brought home' to her Self. Consider that phrase 'having something brought home to us' means accepting a truth. Another figure of speech is invoked when Agnes 'gets on her bike,' i.e. is actively ready, using her own energy, to accept the truth of her own behaviour, the ill-health being depicted. And the bicycle is the first vehicle we use on the road to independence.

Agnes is taking a different route home and on this route there is new development, not only a new road but also new houses. Remembering Jung's insight (that the House represents the Self) we see new development underway within Agnes. She is not being sucked into the violent, destructive behaviour of the head-banging husband-character. When we explored this element, Agnes identified the scene as an actual memory and realised the futility of colluding with it. She was thus also able to own the behaviour of this character as an aspect of her own destructiveness.

When we explored the character of Anne, whose house Agnes is cycling towards, we discovered that Anne was someone in the community whom Agnes associated with good mothering. Agnes makes her way to this healthy model just as she rejects the destructive counterpart. As she approaches, a poem comes by text from her mother. We do not know the content but we know that texts are used to capture meaning with the least words possible. The message too is poetry, something beautiful, like the message of her dream. And the most grateful part of the dream is the evidence of her healing when she tells her mother she loves her.

Finally, the character from the soap opera was a controlling mother. This suggests that not only did Agnes need to let go of her own mother with love, but she also needs to release the part of herself that she identifies with this fictional character. The dream chose the archetype of the Controlling Mother rather than other characters from the soap in order to bring home to her (There's that phrase again!) this truth about herself.

Bringing Wisdom to Consciousness

We move now from our survey of the Language of Dreams to consider the reasons why there has to be a language at all. What is the _purpose_ of dreams? It has been said that dreams are the most common means of the unconscious to bring its wisdom to consciousness. Marie-Louise von Franz, who worked for many years with Carl Jung, argues in _The Way of the Dream_ that dreams bring memories, insights and experiences, and awaken dormant feelings in our relationships. They enrich and broaden our horizons. They warn, rebuke, confront and support us. They can also foretell future events and point us in a particular direction since the dream comes from a non-linear time.

She also observes "they will not tell us what we already know, but what we need to be made aware of." In his book, _Three Worlds of Therapy_, Anthony Barton echoes her insight, saying, "By trying to live without taking into account issues that have been overlooked, we are one-sided and incomplete." He compares the consequences for our Psyche to that of an imbalanced diet for the body. Our dreams offer us a unique picture of the neglected or overlooked issues in our lives, but where do we turn to for a guide to the Psyche that indicates all the different viewpoints we naturally possess? I believe Carl Jung offers the best 'map' we could ask for. We shall turn to his account of the Psyche below.

No book such as this could be complete without reference to Edgar Cayce (1877-1945), known as the 'sleeping prophet.' For forty years he would enter a dream state or altered state of consciousness in which he would be given guidance on all matters relating to life. From the many thousands of recorded readings Cayce gave, his credence of dream wisdom is evident. His readings suggest that we find the influence of the highest level of mind expressed frequently in our dreams. He speaks about spiritual forces being related to the 'superconscious' mind, patterning forces resulting from the consciousness of wholeness and oneness characteristic of the image of perfection (as described in Genesis 1:27). This patterning, existing as a potentiality within us, is influenced by the spiritual forces showing up in our dreams as direct guidance or warnings to urge us towards that potential.

Dream: Father as Hero

Martin dreams that his father is Harrison Ford, and they are looking for a site on which to build his house. They needed a certain sum of money for the deposit but he does not have sufficient. There is conflict, as Martin had expected and understood that his father's part in the plan was to purchase the site. Then he anticipates wanting red doors while his father envisions yellow doors. Martin is picking flowers as the dream ends.

Reflection: From working on this dream, we quickly discovered Martin associated the actor mentioned with an idealised Hero/Father figure. His real father, by contrast, had abandoned him at a very young age and thus fell short of his basic needs and expectations. The search for a site is always indicative of the quest for an ideal foundation, the ground upon which we are developed. Despite his experiences, Martin had nonetheless formed a powerful connection with his father, remembered being with him and still carried expectations that this foundation would be built upon. He had early memories of his presence and love, as well as of his own love for him, together with the difficult memories of being left behind and feeling bereft.

In the second part of this dream, we see the continuation of the conflict between the dreamer and his father. He wants red doors and the father wants yellow doors, and Martin picks flowers. Flowers represent our blooming and our 'coming into bloom.' For this dreamer, the colour red represented all he wanted in life (love, passion, energy, anger and fire) while the colour yellow, he told me, simply meant 'coward.' This was the first time in his adult life that this man had begun to see that his father was no hero, but a coward. And he was ready to begin the realistic journey of healing, from his idealised projection of his father, towards the reality of his father's shortcomings and his own new understanding of life.

Jung's Map of the Human Psyche

Carl Jung understood much about the Psyche that remains useful to us. His erstwhile mentor, Sigmund Freud, once described dreams as the "royal road to the unconscious." Jung not only travelled down that road, he brought us back a map. His model of the human Psyche is invaluable for us to understand and fully experience our inner world.

Consider first his definition of the Dream, which he describes as "a spontaneous self-portrayal in symbolic form of the actual situation in the unconscious." This 'self-portrayal' originates in our Psyche's amazing ability to scan our everyday experiences and create images. Like antennae in constant pursuit of signals, it converts and uses these raw materials to show us how we are doing on our path to wholeness.

Jung's map describes the Psyche/Mind as having four main functions, namely: **Thinking, Feeling, Intuition, Sensation.**

Each of these functions approaches reality from a different viewpoint. Commonly, one or two functions are more developed in an individual while the others remain dormant and inferior. The dream attempts to bring balance between the inferior or undeveloped functions and the more developed or dominant ones.

Jung also describes the human person as someone split into many parts. On the conscious level we can identify with whatever role we choose, whereas in the unconscious there can be a great variety of psychic dispositions at war with each other. One of the main purposes of our dreamlife is to awaken and integrate dormant feelings and unlived aspects of our personalities. They challenge us but also support us as we reach for, and live out, our fullest potential.

Striving for integration and wholeness is at the heart of psychotherapy, that practise (and this book) amounts to an 'Invitation to Wholeness.' Dreams not only show us areas of brokenness, but when we follow our dream wisdom, they also return us via the "royal road of our unconscious" to our original potential for wholeness.

Psychosynthesis

Dr Roberto Assagioli, the Italian psychiatrist who founded the Psychosynthesis movement, describes the many parts of our unconscious as **sub-personalities**. He emphasises the need for harmony and balance within parts that are often suppressed or denied expression. Over the course of our lives we tend to exaggerate or over-emphasise certain dimensions of the Self to the exclusion of other vital, but as yet undeveloped, dimensions. Jung also saw these undeveloped, inferior dimensions as potential in need of development.

One of the first steps towards wisdom is awareness, and to develop awareness we need to listen. We need to listen to what we see, feel and hear. Our dreams will not only show us how we listen or what we are not listening to, they will also help us to see how we were injured when no one listened to us. They help us differentiate between our persona and our real Self and even communicate to us where the block is.

No one is all-ignorant and no one has all the knowledge. Together we have wisdom.

Dream Sequence

Remember the previous dream about the search for a site? Over time attending to my dreams, I noticed a thematically unified sequence of dreams, though all different from each other, the buildings were all in some state of reconstruction or development. I continued to discover new dimensions or rooms full of potential. Each dream indicated a different stage of progress and reflected my own self-development, both actual and anticipated. Hungry for growth, I was also, at the time, spending most of my weekends in workshops. Late in this series of dreams, I dreamed that I had bought a fully reconstructed house, with fire in the hearth. Prior to this, I had spent most of my time being very active in the outer world, available to everyone except myself, and knowing very little about my inner world. Now, in 'buying the house,' I had invested in my Self and was beginning to live from my own centre.

The following dream demonstrates **the human person as someone who is split.**

Dream: Through the Divided Room

I am going down a corridor that has rooms off it. I enter one of the rooms and notice it has been emptied out, as if someone is after clearing it in preparation for some new purpose. I notice a door in the centre of one wall, and I go through it to discover that the other side is but the other part of this same room. A partition wall had been constructed at some earlier time to facilitate a large family. I am aware that it is now possible to take away the wall that once divided this room. From this room, there is another door that leads outside to where there are trees and shrubs in pots that are too small to contain them. I realise it is time to plant them in the garden.

Reflection: If we accept that the room represents a part of my Self then I can understand why I too had constructed inner walls for survival as a middle member of a large family, the 'splitting' that Jung spoke of. How encouraging the cue to remove the inner split and return to an original wholeness! Giving the trees and shrubs more space suggests that they had outgrown their confinement in the pot, which once functioned as a necessary containment. The clearing out of old stuff represented the inner work I had been doing.

The emergence into the outer world is also significant. In the second door lay an invitation to go out and offer healing to others through their dreams. But this access only became available *after* the inner room was returned to oneness, its original state.

The Two Hemispheres

For our purposes here, the brain or 'mental field' is best understood as two hemispheres. The dominant Rational or **Left Brain** organises our experiences logically and orders them in time and space for expression in language. This hemisphere, which controls our waking life, governs the right side of the body. The **Right Brain**, or non-dominant brain, conversely governs the left side of the body and contains our creativity, which often comes to life to dominate our dreams. In this realm, we unleash our intuitive and creative faculties and can experience ourselves doing all sorts of things, such as flying, falling, killing, and transforming. As dreamers, everything seems possible. We seem to grasp the interconnectedness of things, however disparate. Life is ordered along holistic rather than causal lines. (See also references in 'Marshy Ground,' on page 27.)

In short, our dreams offer us a way of being in our world in a non-rational way.

Applying Jung's four-way model, I found that my own most developed functions were Feeling and Intuition, which indicated that my inferior functions were Thinking and Sensation. The following dream illustrates the attempt, by my unconscious, to find balance.

Dream: Feeding the Potential

I am nursing a child on my right breast. The child has already fed from my left breast and was much more comfortable there. He/she is clearly not comfortable on my right breast and is reluctant to feed from this position. I am determined and know that it is important for my well-being that the child feeds from this side as well, as there is obviously lots of milk/food there.

Reflection: Here we find a child, representing my potential for new life and development, nourished and comfortable with the left side, which we noted above as representing my most developed functions of feeling and intuition. But the dream clearly challenges me to nourish from my other side (representing my thinking or academic potential, my left brain). The action indicates that the necessary nourishment is there, even though my potential Self, as the baby, is uncomfortable and resists being fed by less-developed functions.

The child here is a symbol, or as Jung might say, an Archetype of new potential. This dream came at a time when, as a mature student, I returned to academia. With that role, I was struggling to bring order (left-brain) to the contents of my irrational and diffuse experience (right-brain).

Going to bed I often ask for dream guidance. The next dream was one response I received.

Dream: The Call

I am going down the old boreen (small country road) to B's house with two bunches of flowers. B calls me forward as I approach the house.

Reflection: B is the woman who delivered me at birth, my mother's midwife. It was she who delivered me from the inner world of the womb to the outer. Flowers, as we know, symbolise vitality, beauty, celebration and the blossoming of the individual. The Dream Self is saying, in effect, 'One bouquet from mother and one from me, to say thank you.' And just as this woman had brought me forward into this world, my dream has her calling me forward again, encouraging me to come forth again in a new birthing of my inner world.

My challenge to rebalance continued over the course of the following dreams.

Dream: The Writing is on the Wall

There is something on my walls in large poster-size letters, painted by the children. My friend Ellen tells me it is something I could have done myself, and I agree.

Reflection: This echoed my earlier experience, in waking life, of returning from a trip to the Holy Land to find my walls covered in pictures painted by the children saying, 'Welcome Home, Kathleen.' The dream suggests that it is now time for me to 'come home' to myself.

Note the pun implicit in the dream image also, when the 'writing is on the wall,' something is surely imminent.

Dream: Clearer Vision

I am cleaning eyeglasses and windows with silk paper/cloth for clearer, unblemished vision.

Reflection: The dream speaks clearly, and little explanation is called for. Windows in a house are as eyes to the body. We are all familiar with the expression, 'the eyes are the windows to the soul.'

Dream: Three's a Crowd

I am driving a car with two others in the front seat, and I feel crowded. The woman next to me, and in the middle position, is my Mother and prohibits me from driving as she 'pulls out of me' and is taking my hand. I am trying to get up a hill, but the car seems to have no power. I eventually pull my hand free and tell them that one of them will have to get in the back seat, as I need both hands and space to drive.

Reflection: The main image came from my dream-work with a woman who had recounted a similar dream. In her vision, she is the one in the passenger seat, whilst the one in the middle was unknown to her. Since the woman at the driving wheel in her dream was fearless and unperturbed by law or circumstance, my client was full of fear in her position.

Three in the front seat of a car is excessive, unlawful and dangerous. My dream presents a corrected scenario in which I take control, move a passenger to the back and thus recover the power that the car has lacked.

The following pair came directly after taking wisdom from the previous two dreams.

Dream: Infected Vision

I am taking yellow infection out of my eyes.

Dream: Wearing the Pants

My mother is wearing pants/trousers that belong to me.

Reflection: I think you will agree both dreams are strongly symbolic. They are directly related to the previous two dreams, again hovering over the relationship between the conscious and the unconscious. Cleansing my eye from infection implies that my vision was in some way contaminated, my healing action now allows for better vision.

'Wearing the pants,' a well-known expression for holding power, or being dominated by Animus, asks me to recognise that my mother has power that belongs to me, and as with the other dreams at this time, my unconscious shows me resuming power (to see and to drive).

Power and Individuation

When we successfully integrate our conscious and unconscious elements, or to put it another way, balance out the four functions of our Psyche, we reach a stage Jung calls **Individuation**. Once individuated, we become autonomous and no longer as identified with our parents, completing a psychological journey begun as infants. For healthy individuation it is necessary to take power into our own hands. Teenage struggles and battles with parents commonly result from the attempt to make this transition. Ideally, parents gradually cede power to their children as they develop, allowing them to integrate their natural instinctive powers on the road to adulthood.

In real life, this process can often be thwarted or interrupted. The thoughts, beliefs and attitudes that any family, community or culture impart on a rising generation can be good and healthy for modelling, or the opposite. However, the struggle to individuate is natural and should be supported. Happily we live in a time where access to positive worldviews is readily available and visible.

The following dream came after having been out for a meal with my friend. The dream scene is a particular restaurant where we had dined in waking life, a noteworthy context in the Language of Dreams, for what the dream message or support might be.

Note that 'Beestings' is a name in Ireland we give to the first milk from the cow for her new calf. It is equivalent to colostrum from a mother's breast when she gives birth.

Dream: Food for Thought

I am in a restaurant with a friend and we are being served beestings with wine. We have been in conversation over dinner about Dr George G. Ritchie's book, Return from Tomorrow, *an account of his experiences about life after death, a subject that we were both intrigued by.*

The next part of the dream shows me in a castle, and I know, I have been here before. I am trying to pull myself up from the conversation with my friend about the year of the Aquarian. There is development going on and it is difficult to get to a higher level, but there is evidence of progress. There is a narrow passage to get through to get to the next level.

Reflection: The dream is telling me that the conversation we are feeding from as we dine is not the norm and suggests that we are 'new-born' in the area of our conversation. The dream also seems to affirm the development of our thinking, as if to say that we were here before. In this context I took it to mean other lives, as the book and topic of conversation suggest.

Reference to the year of Aquarius could have been about the promise of the peace that was to come when the moon is in the seventh house. This new age was expected to bring harmony, visions, dreams and mystical revelations to liberate the mind.

Another symbol, the narrow passage, seems to suggest a birth canal to get to the next level, again supporting the continuing levels of life after life.

Just as it was not the norm to be served 'beestings' in a restaurant, it was not the norm to believe in past lives and reincarnation in our

Roman Catholic upbringing. (*Return from Tomorrow* was the first book that had fed my instinct on this topic many years ago.) Neither is it the norm for mother's milk to be given to anyone other than to its own offspring. This may not be obvious when it comes to dairy, which we have consumed for millennia, but there is evidence that humans do not have the appropriate digestive enzymes for cow's milk. It is difficult to digest, as is for some, the idea of reincarnation. We do know that this 'first milk' is a very healthy food full of antibodies to nourish and protect new life. This development in our thinking could be likened to the progress from Instinct to Intellect on the journey towards wisdom and the transpersonal.

Higher Wisdom

This next dream indicates my readiness to receive higher wisdom. It came after I had been invited to give a workshop on a Sunday morning about the wisdom of dreams as a means of spiritual guidance.

Dream: Higher Wisdom

Outside my house at the spot where the workmen are extending the footpath, a helicopter is hovering and suddenly comes down and drops a small package at this spot. I have a feeling it is going to be for me. A workman picks it up, and it has my name handwritten on it. I am excited to find out who it is from and what it might contain. I examine it and notice it was first wrapped in bubble wrap, suggesting something needed protection inside.

Reflection: Considering this dream, I wondered why something might be delivered by helicopter and not by post or hand. Being 'dropped down' suggested it was coming to me from a higher level. And the fact that it is dropped at the point where the footpath is being extended was very significant also, since at this time the path was being extended to include new development further up my road. Prior to this new development, my house marked the boundary line between the Town Council and County Council. Two new housing developments were being built with the footpath extended to include them. So, in this way, the dream was marking the point of extension to include new 'development' in my life.

I then wondered where I knew this handwriting from. There was also the size of the package. Scanning my memory, I suddenly knew I had received a package like this in the post at Christmas, a little book called *Fruits of Wisdom*, together with a handmade candle, sent to me by my friend Ingrid at the L'Arche community in Canada.

Now I was able to see why the dream used the helicopter, as wisdom *does* come from a higher level. It seemed as if I am now being worked with or being prepared (just as the footpath was) to receive this wisdom and thus become the means to reach others. At this time, I was delivering a presentation to various groups and communities called *The Wisdom of Working with our Dreams*.

Dream: Dream Doctors

Ned is being opened up or operated on by Ninja Warriors. This is happening on the top floor of a skyscraper building. Ned described his dream as a nightmare since he is terrified that he is going to die.

Reflection: At first, Ned did not want to explore this 'nightmare' but when I explored his association with Ninja Warriors he was able to cite a recent TV programme and identified them as martial artists of a very high calibre. When we applied this idea of high skill being applied to him he was now more ready and willing to explore his dream, which began to feel less like a nightmare and more like a gift.

When I invited him to re-enter the dream image now, it did not seem so frightening, and I invited him to dialogue with the warriors.

He asked them how much he should know about what they were doing as they had his body opened up at gut level. They seemed to be removing something.

I asked him which organ they seemed to be working on, and he said it looked like it might be his liver.

They said they were removing all the fear that he had experienced at a younger age and that had become attached to his liver. (The liver, linked with anger, is also known as the seat of fear in some schools of thought.) After this, Ned was willing to enter into dialogue with his Dream Doctors in the guise of these highly skilled warriors. His fear left him, and now in his active imagination, as we continued to bring resolution to his dream, he realised that they had closed his body up, and he could breathe freely again.

As we continued to work with what previous fear might have been activated in Ned's life in the days surrounding this dream/nightmare, we were able to locate the **parallel process**. This means that there was a very similar situation happening in his waking life at this time, arousing the same fear or terror as the earlier incident. After working with this seeming nightmare, Ned was able to not only breathe freely again but also to return to work and sleep in a more relaxed way, after giving gratitude to his dream warriors. Note the dream setting - the skyscraper, the highest level!

The Bridge

Imagination is the bridge between our waking life and our sleeping. Dreams push content over that bridge to make our conscious mind aware and uses the most imaginative means to do so. Happily, for our quality of life, imagination is available to us whether asleep or awake and it is an important requirement of dreamwork that we be creative in our imaginative reflections on the images and symbols presented to us in our dreams.

In his book, *Beauty: The Invisible Embrace,* John O'Donohue says, "For the awakened imagination there is no such thing as inner poverty." Consider the reflection following this dream:

Dream: The Old White Mackintosh

I am wearing an old white mackintosh coat that I have not worn for years. Putting my hand in the pocket, I discover a silver spoon.

Reflection: At first, I had no idea what this glimpse might have been offering me. I became curious about the particular coat I was wearing and began to reflect imaginatively about why my Psyche would present me with this, of all coats. I found that I associated the white mackintosh coat with a character from the TV series, *Columbo,* featuring a gifted police detective who always wore this particular garb. Why should he make a symbolic appearance in my dreams? I realised that he left 'no stone unturned' in his investigations, as he tirelessly worked every clue presented until he found the truth. In my investigations too, the same principle applied. Like him, I also became increasingly interested in and intrigued by the clues presented in our dreams to help us find the truth and to understand the hidden messages regarding our life.

Following from this, the discovery of the silver spoon simply represented a statement of privilege. Columbo had the privilege of entering into the depths of lives in flux to explore and solve the mysteries presented.

Similarly, it is a great privilege when someone shares their innermost truths and vulnerabilities with me through the medium of dream. Together, we can share in the mutual satisfaction of truths being revealed and witnessed so that healing can happen.

To continue with the theme of new development, the following dream seems to confirm the state of my personal development at this time.

Dream: New Development

There is this huge reconstruction going on. There are large, three-level buildings on either side of a road, both at the same level of development. It is all one project with a road in between, although they will come together under one roof. I am aware of how quickly all the rubbish or debris has been cleared away. The basic structure and floor levels seem to be in good order. They are being worked with and not destroyed.

At this point, I notice an old house beside this new development and I realise this has to go. On saying goodbye I am remembering, with some sentiment, memories of other times and family gatherings in this place. Someone is outside measuring the site. It is a good size. The hedges clearly mark the boundaries, and I decide they will stay because good boundaries are necessary to work within, for any new self-growth or development.

Reflection: This dream portrays the development of my right brain (associated with creativity) at the same level as my left (logic and language). My star sign is Gemini, and this is an important aspect, the development of my masculine or Animus, as well as my feminine or Anima.

It is also encouraging to find that the basic structure is in sufficiently good condition for retention and development. I take this to represent my basic character or structure of my Being. I took the three levels to represent development of body, mind and spirit. Coming together under the one roof seems to suggest wholeness. The road between them indicates space maintained between them while yet retaining access to each other.

Notice too how the dream uses structure as symbol to illustrate development, integration and wholeness. The old house that had to go symbolised some inherited family attitudes and beliefs that I needed to let go of in order to continue work on my self-development.

The following dream gives an example of self-struggle and guidance from a dream I had during an earlier time of transition and change in my life. Again, I had asked for clarity and direction about a situation in my life, in this case, whether to accept a proposal of marriage. I was experiencing much struggle at this time and feared losing my own life purpose or path.

Dream: My Father's Will

My father's will is being made and mother is resisting it. I have a small child in my arms who is crying and struggling and will not be pacified until my father attends to her and gives some reassurance (or blessing). When he does, I am able to put the child to bed in peace and comfort as I return to the business of my father's will being made. I am telling my mother that his will is already made, and I am willing to accept this. On the table in front of us, the new will is sealed inside a sand dollar. The old sand dollar of similar size is there beside it but the 'back of it is broken' and there is nothing inside it.

Reflection: The dream puns on 'my father's will' (a play which I recognise from a previous dream). I understood this to represent God's will for me at this time. The mother represents my shadow and indicated resistance to change, which I recognised from my real mother's personality and my own.

The sand dollar is a rich symbol. A seashell, coming out of the ocean life, is strong enough to reach the shores undamaged while remaining essentially fragile and breakable. A sand dollar forms its own unique design and detail, in a circular shape, indicating wholeness.

I remember picking up a sand dollar from a beach in Florida and being fascinated to discover, when the shell was broken, that the centre contains five perfectly shaped dove-images. For me, the discovery and release of these five 'doves' were symbolic of my five senses being released in the form of a dove. Commonly, the dove is a symbol of peace, purity and spirit.

The sand dollar has a unique pattern on the shell, both back and front. In order to discover and release the hidden spirit symbols, the outer, patterned shell had to be broken. This indicated my own outer patterns of behaviour and ego.

We are all familiar with the statement from my dream, 'the back is broken,' meaning that the most difficult part of the work is done or we have reached a turning point. My decision to accept God's will for my life was such a turning point. I experienced this dream prior to starting my studies in psychotherapy, which itself indicated a struggle for wholeness. My dream seemed to show me the potential for wholeness through this mandala-like symbol of the sand dollar.

A **mandala** is a sacred circle within which Source exists, and is used in both East and West as a symbol for healing, formed from the urge for emergence from chaos and darkness. A harmonious, stylised circle, it can be very effective for focusing and creating an image of a perfect whole.

Since this time, I have experienced much resistance to the breaking of the shell. There have been times when I thought it would be a shame to break an image that looks so perfect. However, the shell, which seems so fragile, is strong enough to make the shore undamaged, a story which can represent the Self and our coming to birth in wholeness. If I had not had the earlier experience of finding this shell, my dream would have lacked a powerful demonstration of the possibilities when risking ego-breakage to release Self.

In his reference book on symbols, Tom Chetwynd describes the dove as the Archetype of Anima (which, incidentally, is the Latin word for 'soul'). I also see the dove as a messenger or mediator from the Biblical story of Noah and his Ark. He sent the dove out to look for signs of the subsiding flood. The dove came back with a shoot of new life from a plant, a sign that it was now safe to disembark. My dream helped me to find this peace at the first five levels of my being, the senses. (Some time after this, I had another dream that seemed to indicate I was ready to develop my sixth sense!)

The following insights and experiences come from working with a woman whose dreams were most influential in guiding our work. Some time prior to our working together in a therapeutic manner, Lisa recorded the following dream in her journal.

Dream: The Scream

Kathleen Duffy and I are in my living room. We hold a very precious item between us and it is a circular, gold and shiny white light. Kathleen sees a group of men in the far left corner of the back garden, behind a bush. I am afraid and I go and hide in my bedroom. Later, I go out to tell them to go away and threaten to call the police. They seem to run away. I then lock the door, turn off all the lights and return to my bedroom. I then realise I have no phone and fear they will know this. There is no phone line visible. A light starts to go on and off at the back door. I am terrified and the fear is that I will be raped. At the same time, I am wondering in my head if we could talk to them. There is also a little girl in the dream and she is looking in a mirror and screaming.

Reflection: This dream brought Lisa to therapy with me. The energy we hold between us, circular, gold and white, was later to represent our therapeutic relationship.

The back garden represents the unconscious, the place where we keep stuff that we do not present to the public or have on display out front. The dream shows us Lisa's fear of what is lurking in the unconscious, the men are hiding behind the bush and yet visible enough to be a threat. She is afraid they will break into her living-room, or consciousness. (I mentioned above how break-ins represent an insight from the unconscious that is ready to emerge.)

Each of us is the author of her dreams, therefore, how we cast the roles is meaningful. Here, Lisa casts me as the one who first notices and draws attention to the potential burglars. The dream also shows her attempt to thwart the threatening aspects of her unconscious. She tries unsuccessfully to lock the door and turn off the light. They do not go away. They come back and try to enter through the back door, turning the light on and off, prompting fear and insecurity, symptoms we experience when facing the unfamiliar. Having no phone line or means of communication to the outer world brings further fear. This was later to become a very significant aspect of what her dream was attempting to communicate. (Police can also represent the analyst or any figure of authority.)

Here is another key element from the language of dreams. It is always vital to note **how the dream concludes**. In this case, the conclusion offers, as the only available solution to her terror, the possibility that maybe she can talk to the intruders. In therapy, we remarked on the fact that the men were in the left-hand corner of the back garden. Dream language often uses the Left to signify the past, or what is in the back or behind us. (The Right can point to the future.)

Lisa was suffering from depression and trying to find a cure. Through dreams, her Self was trying to tell her that it was now time to allow in and to integrate the underlying cause.

From our dialogue and work on her dreams, we were to discover, painfully, what was trying to break into Lisa's consciousness. And having 'no line of communication' became clearer when we considered that a child being abused and in fear has no one to trust and therefore no means of communicating their terror.

Who was the little girl looking in the mirror? We discovered the answer when Lisa recorded the following dream.

Dream: The Monster

There is a huge room the size of a warehouse, with many women, like pieces of furniture, still and motionless and wearing wartime dresses. They are all attached to couches. One woman, with my style of hair, is pointed out to me, and then, I am on a bed alongside huge lengths of fabric/material for as long as I can see. All the material is different, yards and yards of it. There is a woman on the bed beside me wearing glasses, and she is annoying me by asking me to help her do up her buttons. I am married to her, and her name is Jeannie. Eventually, after throwing my legs up in the air, I put my hand on her back, and she gets closer to me, and I stuff her under the bed saying, "There you go, down into the unconscious." My hand is attached to a rag doll as I bring it back. I suddenly realise my hand is stuck up inside the doll. I try to retrieve my hand but cannot and am desperate, as I hate what I am feeling with my hand. I keep saying to myself in the dream, "Don't be afraid. It's okay. You will find out about the monster. You have your hand on the monster." Then, there is a mirror in front of me showing a small girl, again with a hairstyle that was mine as a child. She is screaming, and I notice her face turns into my own reflection. I still cannot retrieve my hand, and I wake up in terror.

Reflection: There is a lot of material here to work with. The dream uses the actual image of material to capture the symbolic phrase which we are all familiar with - 'lots of material to work with,' - meaning there is plenty of information or many clues to work with, representing the different aspects and symbols of the dream.

We began by working with the part that held the most energy for the dreamer, where she wakes up with her hand still stuck. In order to get into the feeling of what this was like in the dream, I invited her to let me hold her hand firmly while she tried to retrieve it. This brought up the feelings of fear and terror from the dream. She was now, in the here-and-now, in touch with these feelings in her body. The dream tells us she is in touch with the monster that is inside the rag doll, whatever it is.

Using Perl's technique of Gestalt, we brought the dream symbol into the here and now and had the doll speak directly. The doll told us she had been abused and passed around, handled without care, with the assumption she would not feel, break or crack. Although this did sound obvious, she was not yet ready to reveal her inner monster.

I then invited her hands to speak of their experience of being in touch with this monster. The hands spoke of their dread, of the feeling of soap and water on them as they were rubbed together. Lisa still could not see through these images. I then offered her soap and water and invited her to wash her hands and bring this feeling into the present, all the time paying attention to what was happening in her body.

Along with the dread, Lisa experienced a dirty, slimy feeling in her hands. She described the slimy sensation produced by the soap as being like semen. The energy from this feeling, as well as the ragdoll's words, was already helping her to understand why she was screaming. The image of the mirror in the dream speaks for itself; it reflects the child's terror.

The nightmare of a sexually abused child was beginning to emerge. Other symbols from the dream included the warehouse, a place of storage and, again, a symbol of the unconscious. Lisa's unconscious had its own reason for using the name 'Jeannie' for the woman to whom she is married. In the fairy tale, the Genie in the bottle (note the pun, another feature of the language of dreams) commands great powers once the lid is taken off the bottle, just like the forces of the unconscious do if they are not properly related to and guided.

The woman wears glasses, suggesting a need for better vision, and the fact that the dreamer is married to her, means she made a commitment to this part of herself, even though she resists at first by pushing her under the bed. For the dreamer, under the bed meant the place where frightening things lurked.

Lisa continued to work with her dreams, and as we got to know Jeannie in her healthy power, she slowly came to terms with the trauma of child sexual abuse. She was then able to deal with her life and come off medication originally prescribed for a depression whose origins she could not understand. This woman tried to contain the entire emotional trauma that she was experiencing, while trying to cope with other aspects of her life. There were times when we had to put the 'Genie' back in her bottle!

When a person is faced with having to accept painful experiences from their past, the dream can help since its wisdom comes from within the Self. **The Self knows how to present dramatic narrative and details in such a way as to invite a deciphering, which will open the original wound and allow in the light of understanding and healing**.

There are many ways of working with dreams to help a dreamer discover their meaning. One method is for them to physically paint the dreamt images, giving us an opportunity to express, in colourful detail, aspects of the Self we may not have been able to recognise and express verbally or otherwise. Creative visualisation, to bring resolution to a dream, is also a powerful technique to work with dream characters.

In the following chapter, we will continue our survey of the 'ways' of dream language and consider Dream's best-known tendency, symbolism.

Chapter Six

Voyage to Atlantis

Dreams provide the most interesting information for those who take the time and trouble to understand their symbols.
Carl G. Jung, *Man and his Symbols*

Before the written word, man painted symbols in caves. Symbol is man's most ancient form of communication and the primary language of the Soul. This language of symbol, used in our dreams, unites us as human beings in a way that no other language does. Symbols are instantly recognizable in any language, for example we all know the visual symbol for bed and board, recognisable by travellers the world over.

The symbol comes alive in the dream where the language is irrational. We experience the many sensations of the symbol, be it flying, fighting, swimming, lovemaking or whatever else we find ourselves doing while asleep. In the dream state, all seems to make sense, yet when we wake and return to consciousness, our dreamed behaviour seems crazy and meaningless. We do not understand how these things happened, and so we project our lack of understanding onto them, calling them 'meaningless.'

Of course they are anything but meaningless. This chapter casts a more understanding eye on these experiences. Our first dream, like many you will have had yourself, brims with symbols.

Dream: Eden

I find myself in the most beautifully and perfectly designed garden. I have been invited here and am amazed that I am invited not only to look but also to take and eat from this magnificence. My dream hosts, in the form of the Devine family, have cut some fresh produce for me to take home. I have never seen such creativity and evidence of care. The rows/beds have been carefully planted and are in various stages of growth. They offer me some fresh green leaves with seeds on the flowering parts and, as they began to eat, I notice they are sitting on the 'lazy-beds' that have now changed into sleeping beds. The top of the bed has a bedcover on it that was being used to germinate the seeds and would be later removed to allow the seeds to take deeper root in the soil.

At this point, all the other members of the Devine family come into the garden from the right. The mother comes towards me with a bowl of fresh fruit and vegetables from the garden and offers it to me as we embrace. Another member takes from the bowl one particular piece of vegetable, and as we examine it, she notices that it looked somewhat like a courgette with roots that look like seaweed. Its centre has become soft and is filled with fluid. Though firm on the outside, she instructs that it should be gently squeezed into the soil so that the fluid can seed it.

As the sisters examine the roots that look like seaweed or octopus legs, they realise one of them has used this design and recreated it on the bottom of the bridal dress for her sister, who is also present. The children are engaging with their mother, who is totally present and enjoying them. One child, called Grace, seems at first to be observing or taking in all that is happening, and as I embrace her, she gets involved in the gardening with everyone. The atmosphere is celebratory.

At this point the table was prepared and I am invited to sit with all of the Devine family for the banquet from, and in, this garden. At first I feel unworthy but they insist that there is a place for everyone and indeed, respect for everyone's difference and gift. The chair they offer me is my father's chair, wooden, with back and side supports in a circular shape - the chair of authority.

Reflection: The opening scene features an invitation to the perfect garden. There is a touch of Genesis here. This is no ordinary garden but a perfect one. Much work has been done to get it in such order, thanks to a family whose name happens to be Devine, punning on the word 'Divine.' They have worked hard, yielding all sorts of healthy fruits and vegetables in various stages of maturity.

Among the many symbols, we find lazy-beds turning into real beds with the perfection of the upper layer, or cover, being used to germinate the seeds. Look at what happens while we sleep in our own beds, don't the 'seeds' from our dreams come from one layer (the unconscious) to another (the conscious) in the hope of taking deeper root in our waking lives?

The next part of the dream offers the fruits and vegetables and, as we eat, the parents enter offering a bowl with the gesture of an embrace. There is the invitation to embrace the fruits, again reminding us of the invitation in the Garden of Eden. Notice here the seeds are on the *flowering* part, which suggests that when we come to bloom, it is either time to feed others or to plant the new seed. At this point, another member of the family comes and picks out one particular piece of fruit or vegetable from the bowl, phallic in shape like a courgette and she begins to show me how to understand and use it. I had met this woman a couple of weeks before this dream, and, in that waking-world encounter, she had encouraged me to find my own particular way of writing. Here we can see that the 'seeds' of that conversation have flourished in the unconscious. She shows me how to plant this vegetable, not from seeds but from the mushy liquid that comes from its phallic shape. She explains how it must be gently squeezed into the soil. The feminine is like the earth, the womb is like fertile soil/soul. It was as if the seeds of our conversation had fallen on the fertile soil of my unconscious and creatively re-presented itself to me through my dream.

No detail in a dream is insignificant. Consider the seaweed-like root. Seaweed, consciously cultivated, is a rich source of food from the sea. The sea or ocean symbolically refers, in dream language, to the unconscious. The dream also suggests that these roots are edible, in other words, 'food for thought,' and thus an invitation to digest the nourishment from the ocean or unconscious. The sisters too have a symbolic relation. They stand for the many parts of the Feminine and they have used this very pattern of the nourishing root on the bride's dress. The bride represents the aspect of the Feminine ready to integrate with the groom or Masculine, the coming together of the two genders therefore, in the union, or at least the attempt to integrate the opposites within ourselves.

At this point in the dream, there are three generations of the Devine family in the garden, children, parents and grandparents, all present and active, and there is engagement with each other. The transcript describes a 'celebratory' atmosphere. Grace, the child, is watching what is going on and becomes involved, suggesting a wonderful benevolence to encourage and shelter our lives!

When the invitation is extended to sit at the banquet table my initial feeling is unworthiness. Happily the image of my father's chair, makes me realise just how supported I am in my life at this time. Finally, I am ready to accept my place at the table of the 'Divine' plan, and like my father, speak with authority on the matters with which I have been entrusted.

Free Association

Sigmund Freud developed the idea of **free association** as a method of working with dream symbols. In this approach, one simply explores the associations one might have with the given word or image, no matter how lateral or even odd that link seems. You can see the approach at work in the response to this short dream.

Dream: Pearls for the Journey

I am picking pearls from a tree growing in a swampy area. I seem to know that I am to go on a journey or voyage by sea and take these pearls with me to foreign places.

Reflection: I first associated the pearls with wisdom. I then associated them with the oyster that had been wounded, and as a result, developed the pearl that was to be sought for a great price. The pearls we prize so highly are in fact formed from a parasite or grain of grit that enters into the mantle of the oyster. The oyster, in an attempt to cope with this invasion, coats the invasive irritant with a secretion called nacre, which, over many layers, forms the pearl.

In other words, I understand that the oyster that is *not* wounded does *not* develop a pearl, a stimulating idea.

Also, note the reappearance of the ocean-as-unconscious symbol, in order to find the oyster with the pearl one has to first go into the depths.

******

In the first dream of this chapter, we found symbolic meaning expressed in the very name of the host family. There is a similar manoeuvre in this dream.

Dream: Knock and the Door Shall be Opened

I am knocking on the door of one of my neighbours, the Felans, for something they have that I need. I have just come back from a burial, where we have laid to rest someone from the community who had represented inappropriate ego behaviour.

Reflection: The surname of this family on whose door I knock is Felan, a pun on the word 'feeling.' After this family appeared in my dreams a few times, I realised the association with the name, and I was able to see that what I needed, according to the Gestalt approach, was to take notice of what I was feeling.

Unmet Needs and Original Wounds

To survive our original wounds, we suppress many aspects of our authentic or original selves, most often our sexuality, instinctive nature and creative imagination. However, life has an uncanny way of reopening those wounds through the people we meet. We tend to find a partner or friends onto whom we project the desire to have those unmet needs satisfied.

When this proves difficult or does not happen, we can end up shaping our children to supply those needs. However, for the purpose of healing, our dreams are most efficient at making the connections we need to acknowledge.

The next short dream proved to be a challenging gift and also inspired the title of this book.

Dream: The River of Life

I am in a river, yet this river is like a theatre where I am seeing, being and recognising all the scenes from another time or place. It is as if the scenes are the same, although the characters are different. Same play, different actors! As I wake up, I am amazed at this glimpse or insight.

Reflection: If I am to be the river, I am ever-changing and alive with the drama of all the life that goes on in and around me. I am new water, ever-flowing over old rocks and leaving subtle changes in my wake. Twigs and debris get caught up in me at times, and I can be both gentle and furious as I make my way towards my destination. My destination is the ocean, which, as we have seen, symbolises the unconscious realm.

I am also at the mercy of how humankind will manage the other elements that cause me to exist. For me to continue existing, I need this beautiful planet to continue to support trees, forests and mountains. I am but the result and return of what has gone before me and, in turn, will one day become a life source for the cycle of life to continue. I am a vital source of life for every plant and animal and human in my immediate surroundings and sometimes for many miles around.

As I was writing these words, I had the privilege of a visit from a dear friend and her children. Happy to take a break, I ask her nine-year-old son, to tell me about his understanding of rivers.

"A river is really a circulation," he told me. "It starts in the mountains and finds its way to the sea. Then the sun makes it evaporate where it turns into clouds, which, in turn, fall back as rain onto the mountains and into the sea as water again." He went on to explain that "the current of the river causes rocks and mud to get trapped in the wall of the riverbank," which, he pointed out, "causes the banks to become stronger as the mud compacts the walls of the river bed to make it stronger so that the river can continue to flow."

Naturally, I was intrigued by the wisdom of this highly articulate boy and pondered the idea of the 'mud and rocks' playing such a vital role in forming the riverbank. I think about the times in life when we all encounter being 'stuck in the mud' and being (or feeling ourselves to be) 'rock solid.' There are times too when we feel the pain of being 'rocked' by a trauma. Such 'mud and rock experiences' also contribute to the riverbank of our personality and make us stronger too, as was beautifully caught (and taught as well!) by this young boy's words. Despite his tender years, his understanding of the idea of 'circulation' was also most refreshing.

Returning to my reflection on the dream above, I explored the experience of being the rocks and stones and realised that all this water constantly flowing over and around me has the power to 'knock the edges off me' and make me 'more rounded.' Water, the symbol of emotion, has the subtle (and sometimes fierce) power to gradually reshape the toughest and roughest stone or rock, constantly challenging the boundaries of the cliff edge in all of us.

Examine the characters and scenes in the drama. Where might I have known these roles and relationships before? I wondered what part I had in 'playing out the same scenes' and which roles I might have been previously cast. The challenge in Dream Wisdom was, and remains, to recognise the 'mirroring' that goes on in life, both in relation to dreams and to the people in our waking lives. When we remain unconscious of an aspect of our personality or behaviour, we tend to draw people and/or events to us with whom we unconsciously 'play out' the scene which is trying to come to consciousness for attention.

Whilst there was no particular scene or character in this particular dream that was recognisable, the *essence* of the dream message came to consciousness. The 'mirror image' of a dream scene had shown me something really valuable.

Dream: Discovering Atlantis

I am walking on marshy ground, following in my mother's footsteps as she negotiates a way forward. Suddenly, like Alice in Wonderland, I find myself in the underworld of the ocean. Here, I am amazed at what I see as I explore this other world. I notice that there are many paths to choose from. Everywhere I go, as I swim around, I realise that there is an ancient world buried here. I notice the work that once had been done, as there are offices in perfect condition, books on shelves and electricity cables. It is as if I have discovered an ancient yet modern world that has been buried in this watery world, and I am surprised. I am excited to discover that all I need is already in place for me to work from these depths.

Reflection: I took this dream to mean that I needed to choose a path other than the one my mother chose. This dream confirmed my interest in the workings of the Psyche and my own chosen path to go deeper into my own emotional world. **In this unconscious realm of the ocean, I am to be based, and from here, I am to work.**

Perhaps there is a perfect world called Atlantis buried somewhere within all of us where legend tells us it was possible to live a virtuous life in harmony with all. The story comes to us from Plato some 360 years BC and there has been much speculation about whether the island did exist somewhere in the Atlantic Ocean or whether Plato imagined it. In either case, Atlantis persists as a metaphor for how rich a people and way of life can be when we work with our gifts and combine them with what nature provides. Plato tells us that Atlantis was the domain of Poseidon, the god of the sea. This sea-god fell in love with an earthly woman called Cleito, who gave birth to five sets of twin boys. The island was divided amongst the sons and the eldest, Atlas, became ruler.

Rich in resources, Atlantis grew to be a significant force in trade and commerce for surrounding nations in Europe and Africa. All was well and, seemingly, an advanced civilisation lived there in a virtuous manner for many generations. However, the story tells us that greed brought immorality and Zeus convened the gods to determine a suitable punishment. Not long after, the island of Atlantis was violently submerged.

The story, whatever its origins, is symbolically laden for our purposes. The marriage of Poseidon and Cleito could be compared to the integration of Conscious and Unconscious or the union of Spirit and Matter. Poseidon is identified with the sea, the realm of the unconscious, while his mate is an 'earthly' woman.

We use an 'atlas' to determine our ways around our environment and I wonder if it is from the name of the ruler of Atlantis, the first son called Atlas, that we take this name, giving us instant access to routes and directions. Seeing the many other routes in this water world was my first insight from the dream. It is significant for me to think of Atlas as being the fruit of the union of spirit and matter or the result of integration between conscious and unconscious as being the source or ruler from which we take direction.

What a wonderful gift this dream gave me, prompting me to explore the rich history of Atlantis!

In the next chapter, we will examine the wider context that these symbols are suggesting, the journey to individuation and healthy integration of the various impulses and inclinations evolving from our inner selves.

Chapter Seven

The Statement and the Censor

It is so much simpler to bury reality than it is to dispose of dreams.
Don DeLillo, *Americana*

We have been looking at the language of the dream through a series of transcripts and reflections. This language is mainly symbolic and imaginative, and the experience for dreamers is irrational. My task is to find a way for you, the reader, to embrace and integrate a part of us, which, by its nature, is alien to our rational minds.

Our conscious mind always has a need to understand, whereas our unconscious sphere, bound by its own laws, cannot be clarified by rational means. Dreams offer a rich and valuable means of integration of our inner, unconscious Self with our consciousness. Once we are open to the experience, the unconscious realm reveals itself step-by-step.

The Hazelnut

Through dreams we gain the most authentic insight possible into the workings of our Psyche. Why? Because their wisdom comes to us uncensored by the **Ego**. The image of a hazelnut might best describe the relationship between Self and Ego. The kernel at the centre of the nut is symbolic of the Self and cannot develop without the protection of the outer crust or shell (which represents Ego) for an appropriate period of time. Yet this very outer protection, if uncracked, will eventually cause the kernel to shrivel and die.

Carl Jung described the Psyche/mind as the field of all our mental activities, an aggregate rooted in the human spirit. Ego is the part of us that chooses what to present (and what to deny or repress) and refers to all that we are directly aware of and in control of, in the realm of consciousness.

In its 'narrow' function, Ego relegates much of what it finds difficult or dislikes into the realm of the unconscious. Other aspects of oneself, such as painful memories, experiences of fear and emotions like anger, fear, shame, vulnerability and powerlessness can be repressed and stored in the unconscious until we are mature enough to manifest and integrate them.

The wider function of the Ego is to bring about consciousness of our identity. In the first half of our lives we spend most of the time building up our Ego or a sense of who (we think) we are. For healthy living it is vital to have a strong sense of knowing who we are.

Always the function of the dream is to bring integration and resolution to our lives. In the following dream, poetry is used to show me that I should follow through on my commitment to develop my more creative side.

Dream: The Poetry Reading

I am out with the girls, and we have arranged to go to a poetry reading. There is a split in the group. Confusion and indecision come about regarding whether or not we are going. I take it on myself to ask each person to state whether they are coming to it. Some say "No" and others do not know. It is eight-thirty, and the reading is about to start. I resolve to stick to my decision to go, even though some are crying. While acknowledging their tears, I continue with my choice. At this point I notice how creative the women's clothes are, beautifully designed robes with matching hats and flowing cloaks at the back. I am now in the backseat of a car on my way to the poetry reading with a child. I suddenly realise something huge is upon us, over us and looking down on us.

Reflection: The dream calls me into 'the now.' Since the reading is happening now, it is time for me to decide and to focus. Focus is usually associated with the male or left side of our brain but there is no male figure in the dream. It is important to notice what is obvious by its absence. The various aspects of the feminine are in chaos or some emotional state. To bring focus to the chaos or emotional state of the feminine, I must develop my Animus (male side), which seems to happen naturally in dreams. When I honour this invitation, another force seems to takes over. I am now in the backseat, being driven, with a child who represents the potential that must be taken care of. This is the moment when I realise that something more powerful is above us and looking down on us.

Russian poet, Aleksandr Pushkin, caught this perfectly in a poem called *'Autumn.'* A translation of one verse is as follows:

> *"And I forget the world, in blissful peace*
> *I am sweetly lulled by my imagination*
> *And poetry awakens in me then*
> *My soul, hard pressed by lyric agitation*
> *Trembles, resounds and seeks as if in sleep*
> *To surface finally in free expression -*
> *And I receive a host of guests unseen*
> *Old-time acquaintances, fruits of my dreams..."*

An unyielding Ego hinders the birth of Self and we too can 'shrivel and die' internally instead of living fully the vibrancy of life. The womb that nourishes and protects the baby ultimately becomes a smothering place if it does not open to let the baby out.

Carl Jung often wrote about the importance of separating ourselves from the mother to whom we have become attached, in order to develop a separate, individuated being. He went on to make the intriguing observation that we must re-enter our mother in order to be born again of Spirit. Jung himself experienced his mother as dark and unpredictable, "rooted," as he said himself, "in the deep, invisible ground. She knew the world of the uncanny and could be frightening and erratic."

Jung realised the discipline he had been searching for was psychiatry and, on reading a textbook by Richard von Krafft-Ebing, discovered that a psychiatrist's response to the 'diseased personality,' as it was then known, should be with the whole of the psychiatrist's *own* personality. In other words, Jung realised, psychiatry was necessarily subjective:

"Here was the empirical field common to biological and spiritual facts, which I had everywhere sought and nowhere found. Here at last was a place where the collision of nature and spirit became a reality." Memories, Dreams, Reflections.

In psychiatry, Jung found a domain where he could embark on individuation and on that re-entry process he described. This re-entry is a complex psychological process and must be undertaken with great care and appropriate guidance.

Some are called to assist in that journey, trained counsellors and psychiatrists, for example. Jung's journey is instructive. "To be healers," he said, "we must first encounter our own woundedness and cleanse ourselves of neurosis before attending to the neuroses of others." He likened this need for therapists to make their own inner journey (in order to be both subjective and objective towards their clients) to that of a surgeon cleaning her hands before operating.

Therapists are instrumental in 'opening up,' to use the surgical phrase, the Psyche of another. To be properly prepared, we must have first entered into our own process. (Psychology, by contrast, looks at the behaviour of another without necessarily having taken the journey of self-discovery from a subjective perspective. In the end, Jung moved away from experimental psychology, declaring twenty years later that "whosoever wishes to know about the human mind will learn nothing, or almost nothing, from experimental psychology." He said that by being subjective with another, we are in danger of entering into our own disorders, which he himself proved correct when he had his own breakdown.)

Jung found guidance in that hidden life, writing: "Dreams open the door to the unconscious world and are the truest source of inner guidance, because our dreams speak to us with the voice of the Spirit." This concept was confirmed in the Scriptures, "Yahweh said, 'Listen now to my words: If any man among you is a prophet, I make myself known to him in a vision, I speak to him in a dream…'" (Num. 12:6) Referring to Moses, He says in 12:8, "I speak with him face to face, plainly and not in riddles…"

******

The next dream shows what riches are to be found in the unlit layer.

Dream: The Cracked Road

I see the road that led to my childhood school. It has yet to be tarred and has cracks in it. I find buried treasure in the cracks and can hardly contain all I am finding.

Reflection: An untarred road could be compared to a child before ego has formed, or before the experience of school. The hard surface resembles the Ego in protecting the original, vulnerable and pure qualities of trust, play and curiosity, not to mention willingness to risk exploration of the new. Reflecting on this dream, I felt my success in rescuing some of the treasures of innocence (before they were buried by the experience of school) was being acknowledged. Surface cracks offer the opportunity to discover what lies beneath the protective layer, yielding a glimpse of the growing life of Self beneath the static anxiety of Ego.

How can we have access to this 'Speech of the Spirit' with Ego standing guard, controlling exchanges between the two realms while so anxious about what might slip through? The Ego's fear of being overwhelmed by any unknown, especially unconscious content, is genuine. Nonetheless, we must open ourselves up to what is _more_ than Ego. We must go where the fear is, since fear only derives from the perception of possible loss. Without the presence of fear, we would have no need to control. The challenge, here, is to learn how to be in control of our emotions and yet not control them by suppression. **What we fear most is what we need most to engage**. This is where our dreams come to help.

Strephon Kaplan-Williams, in _The Dreamwork Manual: a Step-by-Step Introduction to Working with Dreams,_ has given us a lot of insight and guidance on how to work with and engage Ego. He argues that we must let go of controlling behaviour, and that Ego must risk 'the death.'

This resistance is not simply a crude obstacle but an important function in the development of the Psyche/mind since, without resistance, the conscious mind could not differentiate itself. Sigmund Freud described this resistant 'Censor' as a "mechanism, which prevents the repressed thought from showing itself clearly." Jung picked this up, observing in his book _Dreams,_ that this "Censor will not allow a painful thought to pass through the Ego until it is so disguised that the dreamer would not recognise it." This is a lovely notion of the custodianship of Ego, yet the wily wisdom of the subconscious still gets its way despite all!

Freud had another useful metaphor for our purposes, describing the unconscious as the basement of a house, populated by disreputable characters in hiding who are afraid to come out in the daytime. When they dare to emerge, the guard (or Ego) on duty sends them back down, telling them they are unfit to enter or mingle with the household and the guests. Then they go back down to disguise themselves sufficiently to bypass the guard when he is asleep or off-duty. Asleep, our Censor is off-guard and messages from the unconscious can get through via dreaming, an alternative staircase out of Freud's basement. Strong though the Ego may be, it cannot always keep things under control and gets tricked by the unconscious.

Such tricks include slips of the tongue or Freudian slips. Our unconscious can also reveal itself through imagery, writing, poetry, dance and painting.

******

The next dream offers a further example of how the dream uses symbols as puns or cryptic messages to bring insight to consciousness.

Freud taught us that even the smallest and apparently trivial elements of our behaviour carry vital meaning. A perfect example is the clothes we wear, even in the visions of our sleep.

Making a Statement

In the work of our reflections, it is always important to look for the dream statement. We all know that clothes make statements! And so too, in our dreams, the clothes we wear are significant. Why do certain clothes become visible in some dreams and not in others? To uncover the reasons we must look to the particular memories and associations - the core of dream work - of these imagined garments. In this next dream, notice too the importance of the wearer.

Dream: Clothes as Statement

I am at home in my mother's, house and she has been appointed to some position of importance and respect in the community. She is being supplied with lots of glamorous clothes. They were the clothes of Mary Robinson who was at that time the respected and first female President of Ireland. Someone is modelling these outfits and I am watching. I make some comment about one black-and-white ensemble and the person wearing it compliments me and tells me it was from me she got the idea.

I am then asked for my opinion regarding putting things together, like lace with lace and non-frilly stuff with other materials. I am also aware that all this could be mine too but this does not seem to matter as much as being happy for my mother. I am remembering or feeling less than complimentary about her sense of dress as I did at other times when I was younger.

Reflection: This pretty straightforward dream seems to be the feminine version of an age-old dynamic. The dream chooses the black-and-white ensemble to make a statement. When something is black and white we tend to see it clearly. It is also perceived as rigid, strict or bold. In describing someone as 'black and white' we are saying they are not easily swayed and tend to be clear about their stance. (A dreamer with an overly rigid personality might find other colours being presented by their unconscious, symbolising a requirement for balance.)

Young Mark Twain is reputed to have written the following: "When I was a boy of fourteen, my father was so ignorant I could hardly stand to have the old man around. However, when I got to be twenty-one, I was astonished at how much he had learned in seven years."

In this dream, there are many different outfits to choose from and it seems as if the statement is about my growing up, or into, a new appreciation of my mother's creativity and what she had achieved. I am also led to see her in a wider dimension outside the home, that of community.

The lace seems to represent finer, more delicate qualities, and I am being consulted about what to put together. Separating lace from 'frilly stuff' and keeping lace with lace, could be about putting my own delicate, sensitive and intricate nature with its own kind rather than in company that might detract. 'No frills' means nothing pompous or frivolous, which certainly does not suit me.

The presence of Ireland's first female President, Mary Robinson, suggests my progress in accepting the function of the feminine as an identity worthy of honour and respect both in the community and my own Psyche.

Note the Irish proverb: "Many an Irish property was increased by the lace of a daughter's petticoat."

Chapter Eight

Images and Archetypes

*All would be well
Could we but give us wholly to the dreams
And get into their world that to the sense
Is shadow...*
William Butler Yeats, *'The Shadowy Waters'*

Only in darkness can men fully be themselves.
Michelangelo

'Archetype' is a powerful model in our Psyche, specifically the male and female sides of our character, and so important to keep in balance.

When working with a dream, we look with special care at their origins. The 'Maker' knows us intimately after all and has access to all that we have experienced. With sometimes startling efficiency, our unconscious uses the most effective means to achieve intimate contact with us. The next dream furnishes a perfect example.

Dream: Paddle Your Own Canoe/Taking a Stand

There is some sort of test or exam taking place in which we all have to paddle a canoe. There seems to be only one oar, and there are rocks in the water. The task is to try and steer clear of the rocks, and it seems difficult.

In the next part of the test we are each given six bulbs or seeds, and we are to plant them in a ridge that is made in a river. The difficulty is that we do not know where the others have planted theirs, and we are to try and avoid overcrowding in the one area. In the third part of the dream, I am back from somewhere and about to start my day's work. There is a male guide and someone else who is unknown to me. I am led into a room as I get up to make a start with my work, where I find a gift with my name on it in the form of a stand. The gift is from this guide with my name beautifully written on a brooch that is in the shape of a stand or lectern.

Reflection: To 'paddle your own canoe' is a well-known phrase about making it on our own, in our own individual way or becoming independent. The rocks in the water, then, are the dangers to be avoided on the journey or river of life, also symbolic of the emotional journey we undertake.

The second part of the dream takes us onto the 'river of life' where we encounter challenges. Look at what is required here, six bulbs or seeds. The number is significant. We have six senses that we must develop (not just five!) and not 'plant' in the one spot. This leads nicely into the final section, featuring a personalised gift. This gift, which is shaped like a lectern or stand, has my name beautifully written on it. This image could symbolise me 'taking a stand' in life about this subject on which I am being asked to speak. Once I make a start on my day's work, a guiding force is present, as well as a presence as yet unknown. Such an unfamiliar presence could be our potential Self, once we work with our individual gifts.

Each seed/bulb has its own space in which to grow and develop. This represents our need for space to grow into our own unique potential, not to choose the same area as someone else. What a fertile image!

Archetypes

Where there is conflict there is sameness. If we look closely at ourselves and the other party in a conflict, we often find the same behaviour at the root (perhaps from another place or time in our lives) as that which now threatens us. This threat triggers a defence, which usually leads to conflict.

Scripture states in Matthew 7:3, "Why do you observe the splinter in your brother's eye and never notice the plank in your own?" Our own blind spots usually cause us most conflict. It takes courage, grace and love to help someone see their blind spots, and when there is openness there is transformation and healing.

Often, we are not open to such shortcomings being identified for us, even in loving friendship. The same is true of our Mind, when we refuse the messages, however patent, from our unconscious. Nightmares can then present themselves as a last resort to get our attention. If we have been ignoring repeated dreams and an issue in our life is not being addressed, the Soul/Self sends us an urgent message, so to speak, a final bid to 'wake us up' to some issue in our life. Curiously, our culture has tended to stigmatise fear as something entirely negative, but, as Steven Pressfield points out to apprentice artists in *The War of Art*, "Fear is good. Like self-doubt, fear is an indicator. Fear tells us what we have to do."

Often nightmares involve the 'Shadow' and to properly understand its role, we turn again to Carl Jung's notion of Archetypes. For Jung, Archetypes are symbols of our personality. In *The Dreamwork Manual: a Step-by-Step Introduction to Working with Dreams,* Strephon Kaplan-Williams says Archetypes appear as "innate energy clusters within the Psyche that reveal themselves most clearly in dreams and other visionary experiences."

Archetypes can appear in our dreams in various forms, shapes and figures, sometimes as people known to us or even as vague fictitious characters. Archetypes are not 'off-the-peg' figures that have walk-on parts in our dreams, rather, Jung says, we should think of them as a "pre-forming tendency to creating images," much as a riverbed gives form and direction to a flow of water. This form is never the same but always changing and flowing towards its destination, the ocean.

The Shadow

Among the main archetypes described by Jung are Shadow and Anima/Animus. **Shadow** represents what our ego considers the worst and most concealed side of our personality, the traits with which we are least comfortable and of which we may not be fully aware. We like to think of ourselves in terms of our more acceptable qualities and tend to ignore the fact that in our complete personality we also have inferior qualities. These qualities come out when we quarrel and might say things like "I was not myself" or "I don't know what came over me" or they emerge when we see negative or shameful qualities in others.

The concept also suggests a universal tendency. Human beings have always expressed a dark side in myth, folklore and fairy tale. The Shadow is collective as well as individual, as anyone who has read *Grimm's* fairy tales knows.

Know also that if we live or act out our most negative behaviour, our shadow will represent *positive* qualities that are being concealed. For example, a professional thief might dream of a shadow Self in a caring and generous role.

We usually 'act out' and project onto others our shadow sides by having an obsessive or over-emotional aversion (or attraction) to others who openly display our despised traits. It is normal to hate someone who does us wrong or like someone who compliments us or cares for us. If we find ourselves continuously irritated by someone without a particular reason, you can be sure that's the shadow. Dreams are like magic mirrors that reflect what you think you are or what your ego would like you to believe you are. They provide you with what you actually need for your healing and guidance.

A film adaptation of Robert Louis Stevenson's novel, *The Strange Case of Dr Jekyll and Mr Hyde*, portrays well how the Psyche works.

Both characters, though belonging to the same man, have a different function. The more caring and healing behaviour of Dr Jekyll comes out in the day to heal the damage and havoc that Mr Hyde (representing the shadow side of his behaviour) has wrought during the night. In the story, you may remember that Dr Jekyll, a respected physician and chemist, devotes his life to finding a potion that would disclose the elements of good and evil in every personality. At times 'lost in the darkness,' he promises his father he will help him cope with his anguish. His struggle to find a solution leads him into the 'I need to know' phase. This is followed by his struggle with the 'façade' that everyone shows to the world while hiding their private, other or more real Self. He then goes through a phase where he pleads with the authorities to let him test his experiments on hospital patients to 'pursue the truth' (as he sees it). As the shadow of his behaviour becomes more dominant, his fiancée's father, Sir Danvers, becomes concerned about the forthcoming wedding of his daughter Emma to Dr Jekyll. Here enters the 'reasoning of the feminine' where Emma reassures him that she loves and accepts him as he is, and begs that he takes her as she is. Her father admits that he is having trouble letting her go.

Even though he is about to marry Emma, Dr Jekyll enters a whorehouse. He becomes involved with a red-haired prostitute (more of his shadow behaviour) before his 'this is the moment' awareness when he stares into the mirror above his own mantelpiece and recognises he will be his own patient. Experimenting with his potions, he painfully realises, albeit too late, that he has been transformed into Mr Hyde, who laughs maniacally at being set free.

In the meantime, this destructive Mr Hyde has trampled on an eight-year-old girl and murdered a bishop, as well as others.

Alone, Dr Jekyll wonders about the 'streak of madness' trying to overtake him. When he looks in the mirror again, his image changes into that of Lucy, the prostitute, and his fiancée, Emma, and he sees the love and compassion they see in his eyes. At some point, Dr Jekyll refers to "the brute that slept within me" being now in control. We too are in danger of the brute force that lies asleep within all of us taking control, if we do not wake up to the wisdom of our own dreams.

To work with your own shadow, write down the characteristics of those who irritate you, then match them to occasions where your own behaviour provides a match. Of course, our friends and family are also likely to have observed our shadow traits!

Shadow figures appear in our dreams in the form of perceived enemies, often burglars. Marie-Louise von Franz, who worked with Jung for many years, maintains that if someone or something pursues us in a dream, it is a sign of seeking our awareness, of trying to break into our consciousness. Nevertheless, we often wake ourselves up or 'run away' from these shadowy figures.

Looked at positively, the perceived threat is in fact an opportunity to integrate a part of our shadow. Irish writer Fin Keegan, in *The Five Antidotes,* puts it this way, "When not your master, fear is your truest servant."

Thus, in our encounter and communication with these shadow elements, we may find they are not demons or monsters but a natural part of our own being. Only to the degree that we *repress* the shadow is it dangerous. When we assimilate the shadow, its danger diminishes. For Jung it was '90% pure gold' and who would not want a piece of that?

The task of therapy is to develop an understanding and integration of the shadow side, a means for balance and wholeness in our Psyche and our lives. To achieve this we must first recognise our shadow's value as a positive source of energy.

The following dream comes from a woman who was suffering from depression and believed she had nothing positive in her life.

Dream: The Robber

The dreamer's house is being broken into, and the robber is taking everything she has. She wakes up in distress.

Reflection: What part of this woman is the robber? Using Gestalt, my dreamer was amazed to discover that this intruder was in fact *a part of her own Psyche that found value in what she possessed*. That was an extraordinary realisation and worth pondering! We looked then at *why* he had to break in, producing another insight for her - her depression from the contrary belief that she had nothing of value in her life. When the robber spoke to her he said that because she insisted on locking him out, he had no choice but to break in, and in this way help her to put value on what she had in her life. Only when her possessions were being stolen did she begin to realise she always had something worth taking.

The next part of my work with her led her to recognise in herself the qualities of the valuables she perceived to be stolen. Her depression was the real 'thief,' and her attitude had been sustaining this thief for years without the awareness of her conscious mind. This dream woke her up to a new reality.

The shadow often appears as a figure of the same sex as the dreamer and represents attitudes and qualities we have neglected. Indeed, if we break down the word 'represents,' we see that the unconscious is 'again presenting' us with aspects of our Self, seeking acceptance and integration. The male character here represents the male or thinking side of the brain, and *re-presents* the dreamer with a healthier attitude.

You will surely agree that there was hidden wisdom contained in her dream, offering an opportunity to engage with the neglected Self. Encounters with the Shadow are painful, framing ourselves as we really are, at our worst. The Shadow presents us with the darker side of ourselves, a darker side will not go away by being ignored.

Unknown characters in our dreams are an indication that we need to get to know unknown aspects of our own behaviour. In your reflection, note how you relate to such people in your dreams, whether you are attempting to engage with them or ignoring, avoiding or running away from them altogether.

Anima and Animus

The archetypes of Anima and Animus are described by Carl G. Jung as the embodiment of the opposite sex within us. The **Animus** represents the masculine, logical features in a woman's character, while the **Anima**, in a man's dream, represents all that is feminine and emotional.

When the Animus is integrated into a woman's personality, she will have greater discernment, self-knowledge and deliberative abilities. Although these qualities are an inherent part of a woman's potential, her Animus is affected and formed by her experience of men, particularly her father, and is as different for each woman as individual men themselves are different.

When developed, the Animus is the natural guide to the deepest layers of her mind/Psyche and usually appears in a woman's dreams to remind her to develop these characteristics. The archetype of Animus is the source of a woman's judgement and convictions. In its negative state, Animus is obstinate and opinionated, using 'shoulds' and 'oughts' without rationale. The more male characters representing Animus in a woman's dream, the more urgently she must develop those masculine and intellectual qualities.

Through dreams, we come to know the particular aspects/ characteristics of our personal and individual Anima/Animus, the various conflicts of *Logos* (intellect, conscious spirit) and *Eros* (emotions and unconscious soul). The 'head' (or thinking function) is the focal point of Animus, in contrast with the 'heart' (or feeling function) of Anima.

For a woman, all the symbols of the masculine, thinking world are symbols of the Animus side of her nature. As she develops her relationship with her Animus or inner man, the symbols will keep changing in accordance with the developing stages. Councils or courts of gods or men are a common representation. An accepted belief or a group voice may be a further symbol.

The Hero's Journey

Each dream can be an opportunity to find our inner Hero and Heroine and to discover and engage with aspects of ourselves that we resist while awake. Asleep, we are given the support we need to honour the call to be heroic and retrieve our personal grail of wisdom. In the dreamscapes of unknown territory and of mystery, we undertake new tasks and find ourselves accompanied by all sorts of characters, some known and some strangers. Yet, amazingly, each and every character, object, action or symbol in our dream comes from our own Soul/Self via our Psyche, itself a vast domain comprising the conscious, unconscious and collective unconscious.

The collective unconscious was a theory of Jung's, offering a broader perspective on our Psyches. His original master, Sigmund Freud, worked mainly from the perspective of the *personal* unconscious, where he believed we store or repress all our personal history and 'data' that makes us uncomfortable. However, Jung suggested that at the level of the *collective*, beyond the personal, we are also influenced by universal, unconscious wisdom.

The collective notion of Hero is well encapsulated in the figure of Moses, one of many who answered "Yes!" to the call and set forth into unknown territory to find the Promised Land. For his part, Moses was motivated by his faith, allowing the impossible to become possible when, facing no conceivable escape and beset by foes, the waters parted to deliver the Israelites. At such critical moments in a dream, we ourselves might be tempted to wake, but holding our nerve and keeping faith, might find ourselves delivered despite seemingly impossible obstacles. To stay of firm resolve in such conditions is indeed heroic.

When we look only to the logic of our conscious world, we limit and deprive ourselves of the creative resolutions offered by the unconscious. Consider the ancient wisdom 'sleeping on it' when mulling a problem or dilemma. In our own lives, we continue to look for our 'promised land' and, like Moses, must be prepared to follow our call as we encounter the inevitable setbacks, fears and doubts of any worthwhile journey of discovery. (Not to mention the wide variety of conflicting attitudes and beliefs produced by our conscious and unconscious selves.)

Moses was willing to go to the edge and beyond. Abraham, too, had to be willing to go the edge of his 'Yes' when he was asked to sacrifice his only son. Again it was at the crux of this heroic effort of will that he was rewarded. Going to the edge is often a feeling we have in a dream just before we wake up to the safety of being back in conscious control again. Often in our dream life, we deprive ourselves of the creative solution that lay within reach just before, succumbing to fear, we woke ourselves up.

The next dream features Moses as leader and teacher.

Dream: Guidance

We are students with a teacher or high priest as our leader. Some ritual takes place and someone asks for something that is not allowed, although it seems that someone else has been allowing it in recent times. I see that we are close to my father's field, and we can go in there. I notice stone monuments or some cut stones within the stone-wall, and I draw attention to what I see. My father, now as teacher, says, "Ah yes, this is what I wanted to show you," and as we explore the images carved into the stone, we make drawings of them and then show our drawings (which seem to have become depictions of journeys now) to the teacher who looks at each and makes some observation.

When the teacher comes to my drawing, he, or we, notice that it is as if someone else had begun to shape it (as if it was not all my own work), and then, as we turned a few pages, we found my own work - a scene of Moses in the wilderness. At this point in the ritual, we are each given a little bag of gifts with our names on it. Each bag contains many little symbols of our individual gifts, and from our bag of gifts, we are to choose one gift from our bag to be placed carefully and discreetly in the bag of another. The teacher, who now looks like an older man with white hair and a beard, is sitting in my group and he chooses to share his gift with me as I share my gift with him. At first, I am of two minds about what I will give him, either a ring with the image of an open-mouthed gargoyle engraved into it (which I notice has one tooth or fang broken) or this other silver symbol of a treasure trove. I somehow decide to give him the treasure trove and place it carefully in his bag.

At this time of exchange, I notice that this teacher/master placed something in what he at first thought was my bag but quickly realised was the wrong bag. As he quickly took it back and placed it this time in my bag, I noticed the silver chain coming from it. The task of the ritual at this point is to discover which gifts we already had in our bags and which ones were added. As we exchanged gifts we kissed briefly and tenderly. At this point the ritual is complete, except to discover which new gift we have received. I discover that the gift I just received was a silver pendant with a beautiful blue/green stone or bulb in its centre that seems to light up. It is on a silver chain.

Now, the Master is looking at my painting again, and as he makes some small adjustment, I notice how the bright white light/aura/ outline of my Moses figure looks like my Guide/Master/Teacher and I tell him this.

Reflection: The dream starts out showing me the fact that I am a student, indicated by the educational situation. The fact that something 'not allowed' is being asked for suggests the courage to go beyond the usual boundaries and take a risk.

Moses received the Ten Commandments and wrote them on stone slabs. In this dream, the scene (from carvings on stone) is turned into my journey, and as my dream teacher looks at what I present, it is interesting to note the observation about the earlier influence of someone else having shaped my journey. This could be my parents and community shaping what they thought should be my path in life. And, like Moses, I too must have said "Yes" to a different call at some earlier stage. The dream shows, after a few pages, where I was 'doing my own work' (reflected in the wilderness scene). And indeed, it has felt like a wilderness experience many times as I struggled to find my way through unknown territory.

The dream offers both ritual and gift, and my task is to find out which gifts I already have in my life, which ones I offer to others and which ones I receive from others. The function of ritual is to take us through the transitions of ordinary life into another dimension, an event in which, as Paul Rebillot said, "The universal patterns penetrate and fertilise everyday life."

The image of the open-mouthed gargoyle comes from having attended a workshop with Rebillot (the founder of the Gestalt school of experiential training in Europe) called 'The Hero's Journey,' where we explored the symbolism of the carvings on ancient church structures, carvings which vividly depict the struggle of Hero and Demon.

My dream obviously used this raw material in order to integrate my personal story/journey with universal wisdom of the history of the human Psyche.

Two Levels of the Self

When the shadow Anima/Animus is integrated into our personality, the Archetype of Self begins to emerge. The Self, in Jung's model, is the ideal or true Self in the highest potential that an individual is capable of achieving and communicates itself to us through our dreams. Initially, the Self might portray itself in the form of a vague figure of potential, standing somewhere in the future or before us. At first, this image will be of the same sex as the dreamer, later it will become a symbol of wholeness, including, as Tom Chetwynd states in *Dictionary for Dreamers,* all aspects of the many sides of Self "past and future, active and passive, creative and receptive."

Roberto Assagioli, who developed the invaluable idea of psychosynthesis, describes the Self at two levels, the **Personal and Transpersonal.** He sees the Personal as the 'point of pure Self awareness,' the part of ourselves that does not change. We change our mind many times. We change what we feel and even our cells change and recreate themselves but the Self remains the same and observes all the other levels. Assagioli describes the Self as the "core of our being," the meeting point between conscious and unconscious, the constellation of attitudes and feelings we have about ourselves.

The ego, as stated, is at the centre of consciousness and the Self is at the core of the totality of our being. The function of the Self is to direct and coordinate the various elements of our personality - our feelings, sensations and thoughts - and bring them into the unity of an organic wholeness.

The Transpersonal Self dwells at a higher level. Assagioli says that identification with this higher Self is the mark of spiritual fulfilment.

The Personal and Transpersonal selves are, in fact, the same reality experienced at different levels, a true essence beyond all masks and conditioning. When we are in touch with the wholeness of Self it becomes like the image of God within us, "the unknown and unknowable quality of human nature itself," according to Tom Chetwynd. The symbol of Self in our dreams will vary for each of us but will always be recognisable through the immense significance attached by the dreamer.

Incidentally, **circles, rings or mandalas** are also dream symbols of the Self. The circle represents all that is ideal and whole, having no beginning or end. It is a symbol of perfection or God, as the wise builders of gothic cathedrals understood when they gave rose windows a dominant position. A mandala is a healing circle, (described in more detail on page 86) symbolising the urge to emerge from chaos and darkness. At the centre of the mandala is the source out of which it is born. Such designs help us experience the mystery and power of a centre within us that longs for harmony.

Another Animus dream:

Dream: Catching a Glimpse

We're in a place like a hospital, even though we are not sick as such. There is a man who seems very talented, and he is painting all sorts of faces on the wall. I am amazed at his gift and tell him he has an incredible gift flowing from his hands. In the bed beside me there is a man creating something out of a newspaper, but he is not finding it as easy as it looks. On the wall, he makes a sketch and says something about it being "a difficult one." It shows people lying in different positions. I ask him to paint a portrait of me.

He looks at me for a brief moment, and then, without looking back, he completes my picture on the wall. I have a towel or scarf around my neck and am both amazed and disturbed that he could capture me in just one look. What disturbs me is the fact that I see the expression of a woman who poses on my face (my shadow). As I become aware of this, I come alive and change my expression and became real. Eventually, I am pleased with what I see.

At this point, I am no longer on the wall but can see myself in the mirror of a car whose driver reaches back and holds my hand. It feels good that he (the driver) can see me in my shadow state and can still have contact with me. I am in the back seat and look like the picture he had first drawn on the wall.

Reflection: The hospital setting (remember the importance of an opening scene) suggests that we need healing, even though we do not feel sick.

The theme of recognition runs through the action, most pointedly where the Animus figure is showing me how to recognise my shadow. Earlier, the man with the newspaper is *reporting* the news instead of *recognising* himself in it. This is where recognition becomes more difficult than it looks, where we are asked to see in ourselves what we least like in others. The scarf/towel around my neck could be about covering up the throat area, which is the *chakra* for expression. (A chakra is an energy centre in our body, as identified by Hindu spiritual teachers.)

Becoming aware of my false pose, I come alive, and this image of the posing behaviour is put 'in the back seat' (where it now has less power) while the Animus is now 'in the driving seat,' yet still in contact with this part (through the held hand) while not giving it power anymore.

This is an example of the healthy function of Animus in relation to, as opposed to 'in control of,' the feminine principle.

Dream: Dining at Lord's Table

*My friend, Thomas Judge, is introducing me to Lord Burke as we are
having dinner at a large table. The phone rings and it's for me. As I
talk on the phone, I put my feet up in a comfortable position on a
cosy chair, as if I were relaxing at home. I am aware this is not
appropriate behaviour for a scene like this in such company, but I
continue to chat in a comfortable way.*

Reflection: My dream uses people from my community in a clever
way to make the statement of its intention. There are puns on the
name Judge and the title Lord. However, instead of feeling judged at
the Lord's Table (which would have been the voice of the negative
Animus), I am feeling comfortable and at home.

The main function of Animus for a woman is to bring focus and
direction to her diffuse awareness. One of the important aspects of
recording our dreams is to note subtle changes in symbols as we
progress on our journey towards integration. For me, my journalling
revealed a shift from the Poetry Reading dream, in which lack of
Animus or male focus was stressed, and this dream, in which, despite
the presence of a male Judge, I am entirely at ease.

The Torchbearer

Observing what the male characters in a woman's dream are, or are
not, doing tells us much about this side of her personality. A woman
should not permit her Animus or male side to dominate, being
aggressive rather than assertive. Imagine, in the previous dream, if
the Animus had driven without holding the dreamer's hand. That
situation would indicate a male side in control of her mode of
expression, dominating in place of relating.

If, on the other hand, a woman dreams of weak, crippled or powerless
men, her own masculine qualities may be deprived or underdeveloped.

Such a woman is often attracted to such men in the outer world of her relationships. The following dream symbolises an overpowering feminine side.

Dream: The Jeweller's Shop

A man is trying to assert himself with his stepmother. They own a jeweller's shop and in the dream I am pleased to notice him looking for recognition for himself.

Reflection: Using Freud's method of free association, I was able to identify with the qualities of both characters in the dream. My first impressions were not positive. The stepmother was overweight and domineering. She did not appear to show any respect to her stepson and put him down. She also kept him in the background of the shop when he was not confined to the storeroom. Passive and timid, he had little or no confidence in himself.

The imbalance in their relationship was all too close for comfort and resembled how I was beginning to see my own relationship with my Animus. I had been running a group home for children with special needs at the time and was thus exclusively identified with mothering/ nurturing qualities. There was little or no respect for my masculine, thinking or academic qualities.

However, my Animus was clearly looking for recognition, and encouragingly, the feminine side was beginning to listen. Another positive sign was the setting, a jeweller's, filled with many gifts of good quality and high value and the place where they both work. Consider the casting - the male character's function is to bring out the contents or treasures from the storerooms for presentation, through the woman, to the public. This is an example of the true function of Animus as described by Irene Claremont de Castillejo in *Knowing Woman*. She compares the Animus with a torchbearer who throws light onto the myriad of jewels that are hers in the innate knowing of her diffuse awareness.

This image of the torchbearer presents itself in the following dream.

Dream: The Threshold

There is a whole lot of development work taking place on the top floor of a building where I used to have a flat. I meet the workman and ask him what they are doing. He invites me up to see the progress, and I have a torch or light in my hand as I go upstairs to this higher level. He tells me about the new floor he has put in, although there is still some evidence of the old supports.

As we come to the top of the stairs and approach the door to enter, I realise my light is stronger than what is already there. It is a little difficult to get through the doorway, but as I do I announce, "I have come over the threshold."

My teacher, Úna, is there, and she acknowledges me. The place is much bigger than it used to be, and the workman, whom I seem to know, shows me that there is a cot for the baby here also. This is the baby I was breast-feeding in the earlier dream. Úna, observing what is being done, seems to approve. However, the workman shows me there is still quite a bit of work to be done as he reminds me of the state it was in when I lived there at an earlier time.

I have a good feeling when I awaken.

Reflection: Well might I feel satisfied after this dream! My 'old flat' or old Self, as Jung has helped us recognise, is being expanded with a new foundation leading in to where new work is taking place. The scene dramatises a recognition of the work I am doing in my life at this time. Úna, a teacher, represents my ideal Self while the baby is my potential Self, being nourished by me. And the torchbearer exemplifies the Animus' function, shining light on work being done, as well as what still needs to be done.

To go into the dark places of a woman's unconscious (or 'store room,' as we saw in the Jeweller's Shop dream) is to help bring order or consciousness to the riches therein.

After this dream I began to treat this side of my personality with more respect, which in turn transformed the symbol of my Animus.

Dream: Transformation

The stepson (from the Jeweller's Shop dream) is now driving a shiny, new, red sports car and opens the passenger door for me.

Reflection: Easy to see the change in confidence! The colour red indicates passion and the sports car suggests power and image. This dream came at a time when I had begun to study psychotherapy, a subject for which I have always had great passion. I took the image to indicate my developing Animus was growing in the power and energy available to me. The Animus has flipped from one extreme to another, from being passive and timid to assertive and strong. Whenever something is out of balance in our life, the dream produces an opposite, like a pendulum swing that eventually settles in a middle or balanced position.

The following dream shows the progress in this relationship with my inner masculine.

Dream: Engagement with my Animus

I am skipping in freedom through the fields with a much more assertive man. He takes my hand and places a ring on my marriage finger. The ring is my own, one I had been given on my twenty-first birthday. I accept this gesture, and we embrace and kiss. This character is not exactly anyone I know. He is a combination of three different men, all with different positive qualities.

Reflection: Here we see a change in my attitude towards this 'man,' the Animus. I accept what he offers me, knowing it is already my own, the ring that symbolises my coming-of-age, maturity, and liberation as I embrace this side of myself. As he places the ring on my commitment finger, I embrace the commitment to this union of opposites within myself.

******

We have seen some of the dramatic and arresting methods our Psyche uses in its continual quest for balance and how even nightmares have a purpose and can bring us comfort and wisdom. In the following chapter, we look further at the workings of the Shadow and at the Anima, or Feminine Principle, in particular. There is no doubt that the challenges presented by our dreams are many and varied, but the prize is a more fulfilled life, a life lived in the fullness of our selfhood.

Chapter Nine

Further Work with the Shadow

*Knowledge of the path cannot be substituted for putting
one foot in front of the other.*
M.C. Richards

It is not enough to be aware of the work we need to do in life, we are also obliged to do it. Luckily this can be achieved simply by putting one foot in front of the other, taking one step at a time. With that approach we can scale mountains or cross great lands. And we do not need to see the destination. All we need to see is the one pace before us. Psalm 119:105 states, "Now your word is a lamp to my feet, a light on my path." We need to trust the ground in that light.

Growing up in the shadow of our sacred mountain, Croagh Patrick, in Ireland, I have been blessed with sufficient health to climb it almost every year since I was a child. I will always remember my enthusiasm on that first ascent, when I could not understand why uncles and aunts were dallying behind. Curious about the delay, I skipped back down the steep incline to meet them in their struggle and was happy to lead them to the glory of achievement.

All too soon, I have become one of the aunts who struggles to the top! Now it is my own beloved nieces and nephews who wonder what keeps me from the glory of getting there. At such times, I recall the wisdom of Scripture and make my journey accordingly, one step at a time.

The following dream challenges the dreamer not only to become aware of a situation but also to do something about it.

Dream: Potential for Integration

The dreamer, Maureen, dreams about a woman who is heavily pregnant. Someone brings twin toddlers to this mother. One twin seems more acceptable to her than the other, and the mother seems happy to see that one, while she ignores or rejects the other. She then asks for the rejected one to be 'taken out' or 'taken away' as she cannot cope. Maureen is drawn to the one she rejects.

Reflection: This simple snippet of a dream has much to offer the pilgrim dreamer. Note Maureen's feeling at the conclusion. The feeling at the end of a dream is usually the signpost from which to go forward and with which to work. Being drawn to the rejected one is like choosing the 'stone rejected by the builders that proved to be the keystone' from Psalm 118. I am also reminded of Jesus in the garden of Gethsemane (Luke 22:42) when He was so tired that He cried out to His Father, "Take this cup away from me." Yet He was able to add, "Nevertheless, let your will be done, not mine."

In the dream, the given task seems too much, and yet, such a situation is exactly where we need to seek help. I remember climbing Croagh Patrick some years ago when my good friend, Eileen, was about to quit. I talked her into taking just one step at a time. Her joy on arrival made every step worthwhile.

Being pregnant in a dream is a sign of new possibility and birth. The unborn child, not yet ready to leave the womb, is evidence of inner life being developed.

Twins symbolise the dual nature, or two sides, of being one being. Within the word 'individual' we find the word 'dual,' implying two ways, a 'dual carriageway' means traffic being able to go both ways, freely.

For this woman, her dream was showing her that she was pregnant with the possibility of accepting her rejected twin or part of herself (remember Jung's Anima and Animus). We can all imagine the difficulty of caring for twin toddlers while pregnant, yet this is exactly the scene chosen by Maureen's Psyche to offer her this insight. Toddlers are at the age when they get on their feet and find their voice. They, more or less, demand that the universe is there to see and hear them. It seems she had been able to accept both children but, for some reason, now finds it too much or too difficult, and she is asking for the less acceptable one to be taken away.

It is exactly at this point of some new possibility in our development that we tend to negate, to feel what is being asked of us is 'too much.' Jesus in Gethsemane was so close to the pinnacle of His mission on earth when He cried out for help. We all have our own Croagh Patrick challenge, a goal seemingly unattainable, with a last surge of difficulty before the birth of achievement.

Maureen's life experience had been to suffer rejection every time she showed a need or an emotion. She had therefore tried to cast off her needs. The dream, however, offered her the opportunity to look at her willingness to negate, to try to get rid of this vulnerable and needy side of herself. When we worked with the part she wanted rid of, she was able to clearly see her difficulty in acknowledging the validity of her emotional needs. Not only was this a challenge to be overcome, but there was also the possibility of new life, once she pushed beyond the point of negation.

The dream became very significant when she listened to the voice of the part of herself she had been seeking to negate. Her (dream) pregnancy was the possibility of a new perspective, the fact that she was able to look at how she was doing this to her potential whole Self. Now Maureen was able to begin the work of integrating her two parts, which was to lead to her individuation.

Polarity

When we bring acceptance to all the sides of who we are and attend to that potential for wholeness within our Self, we bloom as we were intended to.

The following dream shows the state of the Anima in a man's dream.

Dream: Integration with Anima

The dreamer, Roger, is in bed with a woman that he describes as the last person on the earth he would want to go to bed with in waking life.

Reflection: When I asked Roger why he had such antipathy towards this woman he said, "Because she never stops talking." I asked him what she talked about and he said, "Herself and what she was feeling."

The woman's behaviour stood in total contrast to Roger's who never spoke to anyone about what he was feeling. The dream uses this woman precisely because she is his polar opposite. When we are too one-sided in our waking life our dreams will attempt to bring balance by taking us to the opposite extreme. Here we see that Roger is in bed with his Anima suggesting a need to 'get into a relationship' with the part of himself that *needs* to talk about feelings. This challenge, or invitation to integrate with his Anima, was as difficult for Roger as getting into bed with this woman would have been in his waking life.

Jung uses a similar example when speaking about the function of **polarity** in our dreams. One of his clients, a 'Daddy's Girl,' had difficulty in developing any other healthy male relationship because no man could live up to her image, formed by her paternal experience, of how they should see and relate to her. In her dream, she sees her beloved father as a drunk in the gutter. Her dream was using the polar opposite (her father in the gutter) of the true situation (her father on a pedestal) to show her how out of balance was her vision.

Theatre of Dreams

When working with dreams, Sigmund Freud used a technique called **free association**, by which the dreamer reveals any mental associations with a given dream element. Freud, having asked the dreamer to free-associate, would then decipher the dream in relation to these seemingly random associations.

While use of this method can bring some unexpected and often amazing insight, I fear some of Freud's methods of deciphering reduce the dream to underlying causes and impulses and therefore becomes yet another object, put into a passive position for analysis by the rational mind. The dream cannot be defined adequately by the rational mind because it is an irrational experience and therefore challenges the rational mind, which by its nature will try to *understand* instead of *experience* this way of being. My feeling is that dream wisdom is more dynamic. The unconscious has its own reason and wisdom for picking up on certain aspects of the day's residue. Why, for example, does the dream respond to one aspect of the day's events and not another? For me, the answer to this question is at the heart of dream work, and the work begins in exploring with great care the exact details given.

To experience the dream as a reality, we must specify exactly what the dream image is. Therefore, when first working with a dream, I always ask the dreamer to write down, in the greatest level of detail possible, the opening scene. I ask them to note the atmosphere and any actions and feelings. Then I ask them to continue to record every detail of the content, noting especially how the dream ended and what the final emotion is. We also note the course of the preceding day for the dreamer and, in particular, the nature of their mental and emotional atmosphere as they went to sleep.

Dream work is essentially subjective. Jung compares it to a theatre in which the dreamer is not only the playwright but also the producer, the prompter, the audience, as well as the setting and the various characters, including the critics.

Using this theatrical analogy, the psychotherapist, Fritz Perls, brought a new and exciting dimension to dream work. He advocated bringing the dream to life by having the dreamer tell the dream in the present tense, as if happening here and now. Like Freud and Jung, he saw the various characters and aspects of a dream as representing repressed parts of the dreamer's personality.

Thus, in a man's dream, his Anima will appear in various feminine forms. His Anima is the embodiment of all the feminine forces within him, i.e. the emotional, intuitive and instinctual qualities of his nature. In his dream, these female figures may feature as any of the women, particularly his mother, who have shaped his image of the feminine. Anima may also appear as an unknown woman or mermaid, who might seem to lure a man into the realm of the unconscious. Mythology abounds with the image of the mermaid's physical beauty and enchanting voice, distracting and luring sailors towards her.

Animals that have been feminine deities in mythologies can also represent a man's Anima. The moon, for example, is a common symbol in a man's dreams, as could any other resource or symbol of the feminine that he associates with femininity.

Awareness of this feminine principle enables a man to integrate his spontaneous and adaptable qualities. He might, for example, develop a warm and genuine sensitivity that brings a necessary balance to unchecked male (aggressive, conscious) attitudes.

The Anima usually appears in a man's dream when he is neglecting the feminine side of his nature. Perhaps, for example, he is forcing everything into a masculine mould. When this happens at the outset of the second half of his life, a midlife crisis can result. In that case, his failure to respect and assimilate feminine forces within him may cause him to become rigid, weary and irresponsible, or give in to moodiness or turn to drink.

Neglect of the Anima can affect a man's relationship with women. As we saw in examples in previous chapters concerning the Animus, a man's Anima may be projected onto an actual woman with the disparity between image and reality producing disillusionment. The man, in such a situation, is expecting the woman to respond the way his Anima would. This mirrors a woman projecting her Animus onto a man and expecting *him* to respond according to her internal image. In living out these patterns and denying proper integration, we fail to see each other as we really are, fuelling serious conflict in our relationships. When we expect from our partners something that is really a part of ourselves, we are setting up false expectations. Happily, our dream characters can help us to see this. The dream can help a man to see the state of his Anima, whether neglected or over-indulged.

An example of the latter might be a man in the clutches of a devouring mother image. Before men are free to develop the feminine side of their own personality, they must first encounter the 'negative mother complex.' To understand this, consider that a man's first experience of woman is usually through a mother who meets his every need and wish. She satisfies his hunger, tends his body and caters to his need for comfort. In short, he looks to her for fulfilment of his every physical and emotional need. As he becomes an adult he must leave this warmth and separate from her, otherwise, in the words of Marie-Louise von Franz, he may be "devoured by mother and remain a son whose capacity for relationship is fixed in the nightmare of infantile dependence and incest."

This separation, though necessary, is painful and is symbolised in the dream life of a man by his having to encounter and kill a dragon or witch. This done, he is free to develop his own feminine side. I once worked with a young man who was having difficulty in forming a meaningful relationship with women. In his dream, he took an attractive woman home to bed only to find his mother already between the sheets. Startled, he woke up.

Anima is the Latin word for soul. Jung called the feminine nature of man his Anima because "she animates life and connects a man to the deepest reaches of his being." Once a man separates his Anima from his mother, he can then establish a mature relationship with a woman in which she is neither idealised nor degraded.

Struggle with Negative Animus

The following dream came on a night I went to sleep in a tired but optimistic mood, excited about John Welch's book, *Spiritual Pilgrims*, that I had just been reading.

Dream: Bog Reclaimed to Meadow

I am out in the mire, a place from childhood I have not visited for many years. I am noticing how much work has been done and how it has been reclaimed. This was the place where I first discovered the beauty of heather and other wild flowers that did not seem to mind where they were planted but bloomed anyway. The work of reclamation seemed to have been done right across my path and I am amazed to discover it is continued on the other side of my path. (This other side is often referred to as life after death.)

As I get closer, I expect to find rocks and stones to be picked and cleared away but, to my surprise, they are all gone and do not need to be blasted out. This field is now being turned into one large meadow and is already seeded. I notice it still has evidence of ridges from an earlier time of famine. The ridges, otherwise known as 'lazy beds,' are where the blighted potatoes were never dug out of the ground and so leave a permanent reminder of former times of difficulty and poverty.

As I come away from this scene, pondering all I have seen, I remember very clearly times when I went there as a child bringing cows to pasture and had often lingered to ponder, pray and sometimes cry alone. In the dream, I can almost see, hear and smell the experience. On my path home there is a small, old, stone, hut-sized house that my father had built to house geese at an earlier time. I used to fantasise about turning it into a beautiful little self-contained place just for me. I picked some heather and thought I would take this home for my vase.

As I approach this little stone house I hear noise coming from it and am surprised, after knocking on the door, to find an older man there. He seems familiar to me as I greet him, but he does not seem to know me. I walk slowly inside, all the while thinking, "I know him." Suddenly, he closes the door and grabs me as he tells me this could be dangerous for me. I struggle with him and try to reason with him, telling him that, after all, he is on my father's property, and he is not to hurt me. At first, I seem to be able to hold him at bay, although he tries to put me down, and I think to myself he cannot be very strong living in a place like this in such poor conditions. I then realise he seems to have a fairly large-sized garden inside this place. I finally get away from him and manage to get out the door, but he gets out another door before me and is waiting outside for me with what I think at first is a gun. It is not a gun but something he throws on the ground in front of me like gas or petrol, and he is about to light it. In panic, I realise my hair is caught in the door and is holding me back. Eventually I manage to get free and run to tell a friend what has happened.

Reflection: The excitement I feel when I discover the transformation from mire to meadow is equivalent to the excitement I felt reading my book before going to sleep. I sense that this place is me in some way, and I too am being 'reclaimed' as I try to make sense of my own pilgrim journey.

And the dream chooses the place where, as a child and (confused) adolescent, I pondered deeply about purpose and spiritual matters. Reading *Spiritual Pilgrims* awoke this experience and, I am pleased to see, showed that much work has been achieved since that time. However, I still have to struggle with the voice that tries to 'put me down.' At first, I use physical strength and reason (logos), i.e. male or left-brain behaviour. Note also, that my antagonist (though very unrealistic from an adult perspective) lives in my ideal place from childhood fantasy and seems to be thoroughly self-contained.

Considering the symbolic appearance of hair, I am reminded of the Bible story of Samson's hair, representing his strength. The day before this dream, I had the experience of resisting seduction on my doorstep. Somehow I was able to link that experience with the feeling of being held back in the dream and, by resisting the seduction, set myself free. The situation at my door, though seductive, would have been unrealistic if I were not able to free myself.

My dream antagonist was also about to set fire, in a destructive manner, to the ground before me. Fire is the energy of transformation and can be either constructive or destructive. Like passion, fire, when out of control, can be dangerous. Thus the warning from the Animus figure as I enter into his house, which is also my place of fantasy.

The friend I ran to was, in real life, emotionally involved with someone unable to commit to their relationship, a situation bound to end in heartache. She represented, therefore, the part of me that, if seduced by fantasy, could be damaged, but the dream seemed to show me that discipline, difficult work and struggle were necessary for transformation and freedom.

The doorstep represents the place between the inner world (private) and the outer (public). In *Memories, Dreams, Reflections*, Jung describes his own struggle with a shadowy or dark figure. He dreamt he was in an Arab city, in a casbah surrounded by a wide moat.

The resident prince of the citadel in Jung's dream attacks him, as does the resident in my unreal world. Jung himself describes this assault by his unconscious Psyche as representative of the emotional, primitive and vital elements of his personality, elements suppressed in the predominately rational civilisation to which he belonged. He concluded that the darker 'shadow' side of our personality is a universal archetype, expressing the less acceptable side of human beings. If this man had seduced me it would have been considered unacceptable behaviour, as the relationship would have been hidden or suppressed instead of open and public.

Dream: Being Embraced by Positive Animus

A man from the community is coming out of my bedroom after getting dressed. He has also used my bathroom. I am surprised to discover he has access to my most private living space, but he tells me he had rented it a long time ago but is using it only now. I then discover two female friends are here as well. This man then takes me into a spare room where he embraces me on the bed. As others enter, he leaves to go to a funeral. As I look down the street, I see him enter a car with other public representatives to follow the funeral procession.

I then find myself darning a hole in a hand-knitted jumper. The jumper has a whole scene with lots of detail knitted into it, but it has a hole, and I am trying to mend it so that it is not noticed. One of my friends from the earlier part of the dream points out to me parts that still need attention. This work is taking place as we sit on a low wall as traffic passes by. I am aware of, and uncomfortable with, the black fumes left behind by the cars and the fact we are inhaling it.

Reflection: I first applied Fritz Perls' gestalt principle, becoming the male character. I gained recognition and respect and could assert a long-held right to this place (within myself), a right I was only now beginning to exercise. I was also able to see that some other belief had died, evidenced by the funeral scene, and needed to be laid to rest. Now, with my Animus featuring as a public representative, I could take my place in the community.

Becoming the female friends, I was able to accept that their creative feminine support also lived in me (my house in the dream). These particular friends were, at this time, excited, encouraging and supportive of all we were learning about our inner spiritual world and our journey therein. The dream draws particular attention to the pattern or design on the garment I am working on. I took this to mean that I needed to attend to the patterns of behaviour in my life and work on damaged areas.

The low wall upon which we sit seems to be a boundary wall between public and private life. The phrase 'sitting on the fence' indicates passivity or lack of commitment. In 1989, when I had the dream, there was still a lot of leaded petrol in use. I was uncomfortable with these fumes, and recognising I should take more responsibility for my choices, I changed my car to an unleaded model. It was also time to enact, in my outer world, lessons learned from my inner world. The spare room suggests a place in myself that was not being used or inhabited fully. It is in this very place that I am embraced by my positive or healthy Animus, a space now available for the integration of more responsible behaviour.

Dream: Ecstasy

I am on a flowerbed made of turf, flowers and heather with Fr Tony. He reaches out and takes my hand to lead me in a relaxation, which develops into a passionate love scene on a blanket on a riverbank. We are totally involved in this loving. I experience ecstasy.

Reflection: For insight, I considered my association with Fr Tony and remembered he had sent me a card bearing a quotation reading, "Love knows how to make the best of everything." His personally written message, having shared one of his own dreams, was to encourage me to continue my work with dream wisdom.

I had received this card some years earlier and was not consciously aware that the words came from Saint Thérèse, the 'Little Flower.' When I think of St Thérèse, I think of Bernini's Ecstasy statue of Saint Teresa of Ávila and this links me, by further association, with John Donne's poems, *Ecstasy* and *The Dream*. My unconscious knew exactly which image to use to get this message across as the dream experience reflected the quotation.

I am always amazed at how the unconscious has the ability to scan, as if it were the entire content of our experience, and effectively use the most appropriate image to make a point.

Shortly after this, I had the following short snippet from a dream.

Dream: Veneesha Venus

I meet a man who tells me he knows his Anima and says something about Veneesha Venus. (I took this to be her name.)

Reflection: An appropriate image for today's world is reflected in John Gray's *Men are from Mars, Women are from Venus*, the well-known way forward for healthy relationships. Exploring the sound 'Veneesha' connects us to the phrase 'Venetian Blind,' the window covering first introduced to Europe through Venetian traders. We are all aware of the expression 'Love is blind,' as it can be once we project our inner opposite onto another. The hope for healthy love is to know and to integrate our inner Animus or Anima, as the man in my dream seems to have done.

The wisdom of dreams is invaluable not only to overcome the challenges of integration (e.g. of Animus/Anima by the Ego which, as we have seen, is naturally on guard) but also as a compass on our lifelong journey towards wholeness. In the next chapter we look at some dreams along that path and return also to Jung's idea of polarity, our dreams' tendency to use opposites to produce a new balance.

Chapter Ten

The Writing on the Wall

Is this magic,
Or a chalice of red wine at dawn?
Bibi Hayati

...in dreaming,
The clouds methought would open, and show riches
Ready to drop upon me, that when I waked I cried to dream again.
Shakespeare, *The Tempest*

Sometimes people wonder why we should go to all this trouble to understand ourselves and the various parts of our Psyche. Why not simply 'just do it' as advertisers encourage us to?

For one answer, consider the wise maxim of Socrates, "The unexamined life is not worth living." Socrates believed the purpose of life was to develop and grow spiritually. The world of consumerism concocts all sorts of new products and splashy variations to keep us from the very contemplation which yields the understanding that leads to richer life, the kind of life that is well worth living.

A further answer to this temptation involves not only ourselves but also those we care for. In my experience, refusing to introspect when we need to runs the risk of depriving not only ourselves but also our loved ones. Internalised experience becomes outward unconscious behaviour if we fail to make it conscious and heal our wounds. To adapt the Golden Rule, we are in danger of doing unto others what was done unto us. When we remain unconscious of our behaviour, instead of sharing our experience with our partners and those close to us, we treat them as we were once treated. We unconsciously give our loved ones the experience that was once ours, and this can mean repeating a destructive pattern of behaviour such as anger, coldness, avoidance, intimacy, vulnerability or verbal abuse without conscious recognition of the repeated pattern. As George Santayana said, "Those who cannot remember the past are condemned to repeat it."

A devoted father can deny his child the traditional Christmas experience simply because it was denied to him as a child, offering instead, for example, to take the family on a 'winter sun' holiday. Once you are aware of this pattern, you will see it in many guises around you!

******

Destination Consciousness

In his book on psychosynthesis, *What We May Be*, Piero Ferrucci claims, "By coaching our unconscious we also discover a potentiality for countless transformation." So, how can we coach our unconscious? The word 'coach' means to train or tutor, thus suggesting a relationship between what is known and what can become or come into potentiality when worked with. When I think, for example, of a team being coached, I understand that it means someone (i.e. the coach) having enough vision, dedication and willingness to 'work with' the team to bring about the best of their potential. Furthermore, a good coach will ensure that the team members work together in harmony with each other, forming a whole. The same applies to the internal members of the 'team' of our Psyche. If we are not working with all of who we are, we are not functioning as a whole human being. The work of the Self is to bring into consciousness the many aspects of who we already are in our potential for wholeness.

The first thing required from a team is that they all show up at the appointed time. Similarly, all aspects of our inner team show up in the realm of our unconscious while we sleep. A good coach, in this case the Self, will be ready to notice and work with what is given.

We can take it that each aspect of our character has a reason for being there, although there are times when some behaviour is inappropriate. Just as the referee on the day of a match issues warnings in the form of yellow and red cards, our internal 'referee' uses the playing field of our sleeping unconscious to warn us of repeated behaviours that are unhelpful to our way of being in the field of consciousness.

I continue to be amazed at the analysis of football matches, with pundits and fans watching replay upon replay. I assume the purpose is to get a more objective look at what has happened and of what might need to change and to see where repeated strengths and weaknesses become visible. In the same way though, our dreams give us an objective opportunity every night to look at and learn from the activity of our day, even if it means hearing a referee say, "This is your last warning and after this you will have to go!"

(This might apply, of course, to situations where we fail to make conscious the warnings and continue to repeat negative or unconscious behaviour.)

The word 'coach' can also mean carriage, you will remember, a vehicle for carrying paying passengers on a fixed route. Again, it is important to notice the double use of some words when working with dreams. In Ferrucci's notion of coaching our unconscious, we might also consider the function of the coach as 'carrier' and furthermore, consider the dream as a 'carrier' of unconscious content to destination consciousness.

The 'goal' in sports such as football or hockey is the sought-after position that brings fulfilment for all the hard work, training, vision and determined unity of the team, taking instruction from the good coach. The goal of Self is no less pivotal - to bring us into consciousness, for from consciousness, all life can be transformed.

Morpheus, the mythological god of Dreams, not only visits people while they sleep but also has the capacity to take the semblance of any human being. "Man becomes an I through a you," Martin Buber said, also pointing out that, "There is no true growth that remains purely within the circle of the Individual."

In the same way that we need each other for our growth in the outer world, we need to remain open to the many aspects of who we are in the inner world for true growth. There is no more authentic or better way of meeting our inner team than paying attention to the wisdom of our dreams. The 'I' at conscious level represents the ego, whereas the 'I' at unconscious level, which is without ego, represents the Self and can be likened to the good referee or coordinator of our many inner participants.

The following dream takes place in the dreamer's college class.

Dream: Authority

Catherine is beside me. She asks some questions that seem to be about what to do in a situation where someone is saying they will act in a certain way, on condition that the others would do the same. Catherine asked the class what they thought this meant. I answered, "Blackmail," but she did not seem to think this was the proper answer so I said, "Double bind." This seemed like the correct answer. I noticed two children in the class. They spoke up about the response to blackmail. I was surprised the children were aware of and able to follow what was going on in the class and able to cope.

I was wondering what they thought of the adult behaviour of the class and wondered if they judged it as silly. The lecturer was now tumbling around on the floor. He came so close to me I did not know whether to kiss his ass or slap it. He had his legs in the air. Anne, a classmate was dressed very elegantly, wearing a red-and-black dress with a low-cut neckline and a black-and-red coat and hat to match. She seemed very tall.

Reflection: The dreamer, Ciara, said she could identify with the various parts of herself as reflected in her dream. The 'Ciara' part was her ability to ask questions, instead of revealing fears. The 'child' part knew how to cope with being in a double bind, and even though it was no different to blackmail, this child knew how to give the answer they were looking for in order to 'get it right.' Ciara wanted to trust her inner child's judgment, but was afraid of being judged if she in turn judged her lecturer for being so ungrounded (his feet were in the air in the dream). Yet, she recognised this was the very lesson he was teaching by demonstrating the taking of risks in life rather than following socially-conditioned, familiar or otherwise 'expected' behaviour.

Ciara did not know whether "to kiss his ass or slap it," finding herself in the double bind of being punished whether she kisses or slaps but the dream seems to offer a solution. Consider how Anne presents herself, in a red-and-black dress with a low-cut neckline. Exploring her associations, Ciara saw red and black as dark and fiery and her classmate as strong, bold and daring. Indeed, Anne is showing 'some neck,' (echoing the well-known phrase for displaying courage). Ciara saw Anne's behaviour as bold and confident, contrasting with the more timid attitude represented by Catherine. Wearing a matching hat seemed to encourage Ciara to don her own hat of confidence. To change we must be willing to have the courage to take risks.

******

The Faith Healer

In the summer of the year 2005 I had an unexpected opportunity to travel to Brazil to see a healer, João de Deus, known worldwide as John of God and featured in Robert Pellegrino-Estrich's book about his life called *The Miracle Man*.

Prior to a friend of mine visiting Brazil, I had not heard of him. On her return, she explained to me that she had shown him photographs of those who were absent and open to being prayed for. Saying nothing and knowing nothing of these faces, he scanned our pictures energetically and then marked an 'x' on a picture of me with some other people. We were encouraged to bring ourselves in person for healing, or failing this, to take a herb infused with passion-fruit essence and 'his energy.'

When my friend returned with this news I was, needless to say, unimpressed. I had no intention of drawing on my resources either physically or financially. I then suffered the return of a repeat infection. Though in agony, I was determined to avoid antibiotics believing their repeated use could weaken my immune system. My logical defences faded as I made plans to travel to see this man for myself. What followed was more than I can profess to understand. I simply offer you my experience. As in the understanding of dream wisdom itself, the experience becomes more important than forcing the material to conform to waking-world logic.

I arrived in Brazil. After orientation, those of us whose picture had been marked were sent to a small and rudimentary building called a Hospital for Psychic Surgery. Acolytes dressed in white were holding the space in prayer as João de Deus entered the room, and after some prayers were said, he asked us to place our hands on the parts of our bodies that needed healing. He then called forth the healing power, and in the name of Christ, proclaimed us all healed.

I could hear, what I later understood to be, the sounds of resistant souls or entities being moved out of bodies they had become attached to and sent forward to continue their journeys on individual spiritual paths. This cleansing or healing of self and one's own attachments and ailments was required before we could present another for prayer.

This is not unlike the procedure of training to become a psychotherapist, who is required to undergo their own journey into the Psyche. There we clear out old hurts and attachments (to attitudes and beliefs which no longer serve us) before being freed to guide another on their path towards healing.

Later that day I followed the instructions given to stay indoors away from the sun while the healing continued. This was a difficult task for me, as I love being in sunshine. I fell asleep and had the following short dream which proved to be very insightful.

An old cottage, neglected and run-down, is being worked on and restored by invisible workers. The cottage is completely restored, and I am amazed that no one had seen anyone working on it.

Reflection: The invisible workers restoring the cottage mirror the psychic surgery being done on me by invisible healers.

The next morning, as I took my place in a long queue with thousands of others from all over the world, I pondered how I came to be here and the origin of João de Deus' healing powers. As I reflected, I noticed a room filled with abandoned wheelchairs and walking aids. I prayed silently for a sign that my trust in Jesus was still intact and that somehow He might be present with me. As I drew closer to João de Deus I noticed a jar beside him with a couple of yellow roses in it. (Later I was to read that when João feels Jesus is present he showers his guest with yellow rose petals). When I reached him, he handed me one of his yellow roses as, in his native tongue, he directed an assistant to guide me to another room.

"What does this mean?" I asked, taken aback at this development. "A special blessing," the assistant told me. My prayers were answered. I was also privileged to be invited to sit in the room to hold the prayer space sacred for others. My body had been healed by invisible healers. To this day, eight years later, I have never used antibiotics even though they were prescribed for flu symptoms. Neither has my infection returned. The following dream came after this experience.

Dream: And I Will Raise You Up

I enter a large, holy place with many inner rooms. It looks like an Eastern Church. On the wall there is a very beautiful picture/card/ icon/shrine. I am drawn to it and want to reach out to touch it as it has a message, as on a beautiful card, and I want to read it. I notice a male character from it seems to be real, and it is as if he is saying, "Now you see me, now you don't."

Suddenly, I am raised off the ground and suspended at some higher level, and it feels amazing. It feels as if I have had glimpses of this feeling before in my dreams, but this time it seems to last longer, and I ask for evidence that I am actually being held here. When I ask for the sign, I feel the unseen heavenly arms that hold and support me. The feeling that goes through me is like nothing I have ever felt. It is so beautiful and amazingly pleasurable.

I am then back on the ground and being asked to follow some experienced healer/teacher/doctor, and I follow him up a narrow stairway that has brightly coloured material on the banisters. As he leads me, I see the place is full of people, all of various shapes and sizes and all busily and happily and purposefully engaged in their healing work. I notice that they all have the same dress, though some seem to have deformed hands and feet, but this does not seem to impede their joy or purpose.

The man I am being led by takes me through this open place and then into an office/surgery and asks me to lie on what looks like a doctor's table, and he then proceeds to work on opening my 'third eye.' I feel his confidence and expertise and seem to remember the previous time being less confident. He works firmly with his hands on my third eye chakra and then traces my eyes with his fingers and gently opens my lips.

Another part of the dream takes me back to the office I once worked in. It is the end of the day, and I am trying to balance the takings in the till. There are lots of customers in the shop, and I am anxious about wanting to get finished. Someone comes in with an invoice/bill for flowers, and my boss pays him from the till. I then notice the bouquet of flowers, and someone else puts another vase of flowers in front of my office. We are then outside in what seems like a large gathering of people. I notice a helicopter out of the corner of my eye, and now, it has landed in our midst. A man gets out and throws me a cable that is pulsating in my hand. He then invites/takes me up in the helicopter. I am resisting a little at first as I say I still have to balance the till when the customers are gone, but he just gently lifts me up into it and then climbs in over me to get to the pilot's seat. There is a young boy there also, and I notice someone must have left a long-legged boot on the floor after them.

I am now up in the air and the helicopter is suspended as I begin to take in the view from up here. A higher view!

Reflection: I had asked for evidence of Divine protection, and the dream experience offers it. My challenge now was to remain in touch with that experience. Having my third eye opened, and my lips touched suggests both the opening of this higher, inner-vision wisdom and the invitation to speak about it.

I associated the helicopter with a story about João de Deus. He had been told by guides from the higher place to warn his nephew not to fly a helicopter on a particular day to a family occasion. His nephew decided to fly anyway. Sadly for all involved, and with the family gathered for his arrival, the young pilot's craft burst into flames and he lost his life.

The second part of the dream takes place in (and outside of) my workplace of many years, where I balanced the books. As I took leave of my colleagues to further my life experience, they presented me with flowers. In the dream I am busy balancing the till. Many believe that healing takes place when energy is aligned and balanced through the body's chakra system. Now my balancing must be of energy in the 'sacred book' of my body. And it seems as if this Higher view of spiritual gain trumps the previous concern for commercial gain. The flowers symbolise and celebrate this transition.

Dream: Unseen Helpers

I am at an airport or hospital where I notice there are trolleys being moved about with great efficiency by unseen workers.

Reflection: We began by exploring what an airport and a hospital might have in common. They are both places from which we depart and into which we arrive. (And birth takes place in a hospital and often death does too, both forms of arrival and departure, which we will turn to again below.) Both places depend on trolleys. At the airport, trolleys aid the traveller or pilgrim carrying baggage that would otherwise be too heavy for an individual; in the hospital, they support a frail or injured body.

However, the most significant element here is my ability to see the work of these 'unseen workers' working so efficiently. This bore a double message for me. On one level, it led me to explore how 'unseen' I was feeling in my own work. On another level, I was reminded of the fact that there was help coming from 'the unseen world' through actions visible to those 'who have eyes to see.'

What about the symbolism of the airport? The whole idea of arrival and departure can also be applied to birth and death, and so this short glimpse of a dream suggested deepening the exploration of my own mortality and life's purpose. Great comfort came too from realising that my work was indeed efficient, despite my feeling unseen or invisible, an occupational hazard for one trawling a hidden world. The notion that unseen helpers were supporting me was sufficient for me to continue my work with a deeper faith in myself, my purpose and my God.

The Context of Time

Since dreams come from non-linear time, just where to begin to work with some of them can be difficult to determine. For the most part, we can usually find some clue to the dream wisdom from the raw material of the residue of the recent day's stimuli. However, there are some dreams that simply seem to come from another time and place, and the most we can do is to simply sit up and pay attention (and respect) to such 'messages.'

A woman I know dreamed almost verbatim about the events of the tsunami in the Middle East in 2003. She recorded her dream on December 16th and the awful events came to pass ten days later, on December 26th.

The same woman sent me the following dream transcript in July 2004 and this is one dream that is certainly not to be interpreted by me! Suffice to say it includes references to dreams coming from 'outside' or 'non-linear' time.

Dream about Kathleen Duffy

Kathleen has come for a brief visit. She is hectic and happy with not much time to spare and a long list of things we want to do. A ceremony is starting and though she has come to visit me, it seems there is another reason why she has come (though neither of us knew). Just as we're working out where we want to go (this store, that street, etc.) a huge gathering is happening but no one is there. Rather, they are there, but we can't see them.

At first, Kathleen is either sitting or bending down talking to me, but then it's as though she's lifted up from under the arm and escorted to a different place, but it just involves turning her head. She is, at first, disoriented and explains that she has very limited time and must get back home to do her work. She reacts as someone who goes out to lunch with a friend who surprises her with a private cruise, ready to leave. ("Oh that's very, very kind, but I have to..."). In less than a minute, she realises the immensity and seriousness of the moment, and stands at full attention. I stand behind her, as we both face a darkness filled with wisdom and presence. Many unseen ones are present and there is a feeling of spaciousness as though we are standing in a grand hall or huge ceremonial chamber, addressing an area in front and above us. A voice says to Kathleen, "Are you ready to give up everything?" (Or maybe it was, "Are you ready to give everything?") She does not hesitate for even a moment, but without using words, answers "Yes" with the whole of herself. I am amazed at her readiness and kind of relieved they didn't ask me.

Within a moment of answering, she is transformed. All her clothes have been replaced by these simple robes. She is standing with her back to me, and all her hair is gone - she is completely bald. When she turns to me, I realise she wears a large cross (Is it actually a cross?) that hangs down to her waist from a long chain. It looks very old. She is completely at ease with the transformation, as though it happened years ago. She is trying to help me, and it feels as if she is home, and I have come to visit. She is talking to me, and has one arm around me, and is being very kind. I'm still a bit in shock. I like who she has become, and though I know the person I once knew as her is gone, I'm awed and amazed by this holy presence she has become. All the others have gone. This ceremony ended years ago in their perception of time, even though it was seconds. We are back in a normal day, as though nothing had changed, when nothing would ever be the same.

******

The next dream features a sacred space, in this case a church. The Church, though often limited to material or ecclesiastical structures, is meant to be a living community of believers. I was pondering, at the time, the real purpose of the Church and whether it was serving believers or being served instead by its believers. In the dream, I am challenged to work at my faith as the church/structure of my own beliefs undergoes reconstruction.

Dream: Having To Work At It

I am going to Mass in a church which is under reconstruction. The whole of the middle or central area is vacant. On the right-hand side there is a small aisle where a table is set. I go up there and join the few people already there for the meal/Mass. I am very conscious of the fact that there is nothing in the main body of the church as they repair it.

When I come out into the open, two of my sisters are with me, and we have to go to the bog where we have to work at saving the turf, a difficult task. Although I do not feel like doing this, I know it is my father's will for me, and he is now present, so I know I do not have any real choice even though, at another level, I know I could have refused. Dad is dressed in bright feminine colours, yellow and pink.

Reflection: I am reminded of the Scriptures, in this case of Adam and Eve's expulsion from the Garden of Eden, accompanied by the words in Genesis 3:19, "With sweat on your brow shall you eat your bread." In this dream, we see the state of Mother Church and, although under reconstruction, she still offers the Bread of Life to those few willing to receive.

Having to come out of the church and into the bog for manual labour is the real challenge, mixing, as it does, my father's will and my own choice. Whilst saving turf (and living one's faith) is difficult, the work is rewarded by the warmth and comfort of the fire, which is the end result from the work on the bog.

I took this dream to mean that working with my faith was more important work than following the trend to leave the Church during a time of change and rebuilding. After all, although the main body of the church was vacant, the Eucharist was *still present*.

Note the colours yellow and pink being included and worn by the male father principle - Father/Pope. We often refer to the colour pink as representative of the feminine and the colour yellow to represent cowardice and sometimes referred to as intellect. The papal authority is required to include the feminine principle and also include or display, as in the dream image, the courage to expose the intellectual cowardice of such public display.

The dream which follows picks up these themes! With the restoration of power once held by the church now given to the congregation, a transfer of power is symbolised by the keys being handed by the Pope to a regular person like me.

Dream: Keys to the Kingdom

I have been given four circular keys, made of ice, on a circular key ring. One of the keys, marked 'Number One,' is to the Pope's room. I go down the corridor as someone tells me, "One is the lowest number." As I enter, I find the Pope getting dressed, and I apologise for interrupting as I had not expected to find him there, but he said it was okay as there was a class about to come in. He is dressed in lay clothes. The Pope then gives me another bunch of keys to go to his old vault or some place like a tabernacle.

When I go to open it, it is sealed with adhesive tape but I manage to open it and take something from it to give to him, a small bottle of oil. However, the oil has spilled and is sizzling on a tray with lots of steam rising from it and sending out sparks that are reaching the people who stand by. The Pope says something to me about it being unwise to anoint people with this oil as it is leaving marks on the clothing of those it hit as they were leaving. Mary comes out with a new dress she is going to wear to the wedding.

Reflection: When given keys, we are usually being entrusted with authority or power. Jesus gave Peter the Keys of the Kingdom of Heaven when He entrusted Peter to be His representative on earth. In this dream, the keys are made of ice and are circular in shape, suggesting power in the sense of wholeness. The circle is a universal symbol of wholeness, as is the number 4, representing the traditional four elements: earth, air, fire and water. (Four also represents the North, South, East and West, again representing wholeness.) When I think of ice I think of the North Pole, or highest point of the earth, and a particular way of life. I also think 'cold' and one could characterise the teaching of the Pope at that time as being cold and hard, like ice. We refer to 'the cold hard facts of life' when we find something difficult to accept.

In my dream, the Pope is dressed in lay clothes and expecting students. In other words, he is about to teach from an ordinary perspective.

Notice how everything seems to be reversed in this dream. Number one becomes the lowest, rather than the highest, number. The Tabernacle/vault is sealed with tape, instead of being the clasped and ornate gold door with which we associate the tabernacle. The Pope's clothes are without statement, and in place of the customary investiture, he *relinquishes* power by giving me the keys. Note the principle behind this - dreams often reverse situations to highlight an imbalance and by doing so, attempt to bring balance.

The oil is presented the way Eastern food is sometimes served, on a platter, sizzling and steaming, reminding me of the expression 'sparks flying,' which can mean conflict of opinion or heated discussion. At the end of the dream, people are leaving as sparks fly. In a similar way, many people were leaving the traditional Church because of their difficulty accepting the Pope's teaching on certain issues.

The woman called Mary hails, in real life, from the West and is married to a man from the East. In dreams, marriage can often suggest integration or coming together of opposites, like dark and light, or, as in this case, East and West. Taking it that each dreamed person represents an aspect of the Self, then this dream could be an invitation for me to take responsibility to teach, at an ordinary level, the core message of Jesus, as given to Peter, which is Love. The dream ends with a woman, Mary, preparing for a wedding which could also mean the integration of the feminine into Church structure. A wedding is the ultimate statement of integration, a public affirmation in which the opposites of male and female are united in love.

Looking back on this transcript, the dream seems prophetic. In 2013 the College of Cardinals, presented with an unprecedented retirement, elected a new pontiff. On his first Holy Thursday as Bishop of Rome, Pope Francis washed the feet of a dozen juvenile offenders, including two young women, telling them to "Help one another. This is what Jesus teaches us."

******

The next transcript is such a short dream, yet it had much to say when explored!

Fire in the Soul

After reading from Joan Borysenko's book *Fire in the Soul,* in which she talks about perfection in all things as they are, I wrote in my journal the words 'even me' and had the following dream that night:

Dream: Orchid

I am looking inside a flower at the core of the petals. At first it doesn't seem clear but suddenly the flower becomes amazingly perfect. The scene reflects the sky with Our Lady and angels in beautiful perfection.

Reflection: Like me, I am sure you have been often amazed at the perfect delicacy in design of floral Creation, both in their visible petals and the seeds within. If Nature's handiwork is so perfect, we too are exquisitely designed and as precious and rare as the rarest of orchids. Appropriately, the dream closes with Mary and the angels giving praise and glory to God, the Creator of such splendour.

Dream: Light from Above

A helicopter is flying round the house where I grew up, and as we watch it rounding in on something, it throws light on whatever it is, before eventually coming down to ground. Someone is showing us how to mix sand and mortar for bomb making, and I am uncomfortable with this. In the crowd a naked man asks for his clothing.

Someone beside me reaches out to him with a wrap from a shelf and he is very thankful. There seems to be lots of action as everyone is sent off in different directions. I find a cave that I seem to remember from before, and a woman has lived here growing vegetables and living frugally. Suddenly, there is a large feature, like Street Art, and lots of people are hiding in a large horse or cow.

Reflection: From the dreamwork described in previous chapters, I could establish that the helicopter was a symbol of a more objective vision and also a means by which we can see the bigger picture, thus bringing wisdom from a higher perspective to a situation. At the time, the Provisional IRA was making and planting bombs for use against 'British occupation' of six of the nine Ulster counties, namely Northern Ireland. They wanted to get rid of British defence forces from the north and re-establish a 32-county Republic.

The Ego is all about defences. 'To get rid of defences' could, on a personal, symbolic level, be seen as a healthy step towards owning whatever vulnerability I was hiding by being defensive. As in our historical context, so too, on a personal level, making the dialogue conscious leads to peace and healing.

The setting of the dream shows where this behaviour was formed (i.e. in childhood), and suggests that it is now time for a more progressive approach. Thus, the image of the naked man reaching out from his vulnerability and asking for his clothing, after which the scene shifts to the street artists, suggesting creativity and celebration. The people hiding in the horse/cow echoes the Trojan horse image from the ancient Greek tale, indicating a more creative way to victory than the nihilism of explosives against innocents. Instead of attacking others, the dream seems to show me that, from a higher perspective, there can be a more creative solution to healing wounds from the past.

Dream: Heart of Gold Amidst the Junk

With Mrs Dillon, I am picking up pieces of jewellery from the normally busy main road outside my house. I am noticing how quiet the road is, and think to myself it must be Sunday morning. The stuff we are picking up is mostly costume jewellery, not of great quality. I think it might bring joy to children to use for play. I then find a little gold heart pendant and quietly slip it into my bag.

Reflection: The busy road represents modern-day living, and the Sunday morning setting indicates a quiet time for prayer or time out from the hustle and bustle of life. Costume jewellery, of course, is made to look like the real thing, but is actually made from inferior material. We must be discerning to tell what is real and what is simulated. The world of fashion is a powerful arena for the use of this power. And this dream came before the movie *The Devil Wears Prada*!

"A loving heart is the truest wisdom," Charles Dickens once said. We all know gold must be tested, and I took this dream to mean that having a generous heart (a heart of gold, as the saying has it) is more valuable than presenting a false image. The dream also harnesses the imagination of the child using jewellery for make-believe.

In my waking life, Mrs Dillon had praised my courage for having spoken a truth on behalf of a community experiencing unhealed childhood hurt.

The dream also challenges me to find a creative way of working with the everyday issues and hurts of life, and to seek the heart of gold and bring it to others.

The next dream needed little effort to figure out.

Dream: Our Potential

I am noticing all the extra flowers that I had planted along the roadside, and they are in healthy bloom. There is lilac, foxglove and evening primrose. One tree had been cut, and there was a man working with it to see if it could be restored. He decided that the cut-off piece had the potential to start its own growth.

There was also something about a woman I knew and her mother. I had my bicycle and realised I was able to fix a puncture and continue my journey.

Reflection: I could explore the healing properties from a homeopathic point of view of these particular plants and be curious as to why the dream chooses to make these particular varieties significant. Certainly, it is encouraging to find that the seeds I have sown along the roadside of life have grown and flourished. The man working on the tree that has been cut is my Animus and here I am able to trust his wisdom, confident, that even though I may feel cut off from mainstream thinking, I have the potential to grow now on my own.

The woman was someone whom I had encouraged to separate from her mother in order to begin to live her own life. She was now blooming in her new adventure.

The bicycle, as you will probably remember from your own childhood, is the first vehicle of independence and a way for us to be 'doing it ourselves,' converting our own energy into action.

Vincent van Gogh once revealed, "I dream of painting, and then I paint my dream." This next dream, from Philomena, captures the essence of a functioning creative space in a community.

Dream: The Art of Dreaming

I am in the Arts Centre, and there is so much production, activity and creativity happening that I can hardly keep up. Women are working together everywhere to produce amazing things out of fabric, thread, paper and all sorts of material. An old-fashioned pulley system conveys objects from one floor level to another and across the room space. The whole scene looks as if some super-efficient system is at work.

It seems as if we have all presented some artwork, and women are dressed up in the most amazing outfits they have put together. One is like a statement from literature, and I am on the front page of the local newspaper. The Art Teacher has chosen one piece of each of our works for a show. A little girl plays with a Thai doll. I want to purchase the doll, though there are many more, some not as detailed or as elaborate, or expensive as others.

Now, there is a rare calf born (where I was born) after a long delivery. Also a pony is born to a mare and they are locked into our front porch, with only a tiny hole to look out from. I let them out, bandage the mother and then allow them to come to school with us. I am so in awe of the work production in this place and of the incredible creativity as everyone works together.

Reflection: This dream does not need much explanation. Philomena's local Arts Centre is a place where a lot of creativity takes place and has hosted many art exhibitions, as well as productions of shows, plays and concerts. The words used in the transcript - production, activity and creativity - capture what the dream is conveying. And we see that the old-fashioned, though very efficient, pulley system is being used to 'convey' stuff from one level to another. This system was used in shops in the past and consisted of wires and ropes threaded through wheels to transfer items across large spaces. The idea of a super-efficient system at work certainly captures for me what dream wisdom is about, conveying wisdom from the level of the unconscious to consciousness.

The front page of a local paper is intended to draw attention to something of compelling current interest and the dream is as personal to Philomena as the local news is to the locals. The Art Teacher, meanwhile, is putting the work on show, so the dream is an invitation to the dreamer to literally show her creativity.

The little girl playing with the Thai doll opens up the idea of cultural difference and, for Philomena, the 'doll' reminded her of how girls are treated in Thailand and the unease she felt with how they were 'bought' for the sex trade. The dream restored value to the work of the women in making these dolls, thereby highlighting the plight of the feminine in other cultures and her own undervaluing as a little girl.

At this point, the dream shows Philomena at the birth of a calf and foal. The image of a calf or foal being 'let out' suggests freedom and fun and frolics, especially from such a restricted place as the front porch. Letting them go to school suggests the education of the instinctive Self. This dream invites her to open up to and integrate the variety of creative energies and talent within herself and to loosen the restrictions on her sexuality or instinctual Self.

We have seen that a primary function of the dream is to bring balance. When there is imbalance in an area of our lives, our dreams tend to show us the opposite scenario, through what Jung called polarity. We see that principle at work here too. Animals in dreams represent our instinctive nature, and its appearance here is linked to her birth and upbringing, an upbringing that restricted her natural impulses. The dream could not have found a more polarised image (in Jung's sense) for Philomena than the idea of a little Thai girl. This woman, we discovered, associated the Thai girl with sexual exploitation.

The potent forces at work here take some disentangling. The dreamer's sexually restricted upbringing is symbolised by the young Animals and mothers locked in to the porch and the exploitation of the young Thai girl and her sexuality. The porch is the place between the inner sanctuary of home and the outer, more public, world. A porch is a place to pass through, not be confined in. The dream-wisdom of releasing her fun-loving, instinctively sexual and playful Self out into the world and school was liberating and educational for this woman, but saddening too, as Philomena realised she had so restricted herself for so many years. There is no health in extremes, and here we see the dream proposing a healthy midpoint between overprotective restriction and unprotected exploitation. It was now time for her to celebrate the diversity of her full identity, represented by her many aspects working together in a creative, active and productive way.

Dream: Grace

I notice a baby called Grace is walking and talking and living in my childhood home. I am wondering where I had been while she was developing, and wondering how I had missed out on this experience. Her mother is with her, and she is pregnant. On the wall there is a large sheet of paper, like a family tree, full of details about Grace's life and commitments she will make. The back of the page is carefully designed in blue ink and in the shape of petals. There is a lot of information on the page as if it is an astrological chart reading.

Reflection: Living the life of Grace, what an invitation! And to discover it was already happening when I was not aware of it, in the place of my childhood, and even whilst in the womb! The dream could not be more pointed. Note the colour blue of the chart's background. The reading comes 'out of the blue,' therefore as something unexpected and, in that phrase's usual association, as something positive. Insight from the unconscious often seems to have come 'out of the blue.' Such detail in the inked design indicates care, while petals symbolise perfection and delicacy. My life's purpose therefore, has not only been carefully designed from the unconscious or 'blue' but also presented to me as 'the writing is on the wall,' i.e. an imminent reality. It is time to accept this guidance from that wild blue yonder realm.

Dream: The Other Side of Grace

The same child, Grace, has a twin with blue eyes in contrast with her own green eyes.

Reflection: Our duality can present in the form of twins in our dreams or, as indicated here, in the form of contrast. The function of the dream is to offer the potential for integration and acceptance of difference. In this case, without the quality of Grace in our lives it can sometimes be difficult to see both sides of a situation.

Incidentally, the ancient mystic Rumi has a lovely poem which captures a place beyond duality that could well be that field where the dreams come from!

> *"Out beyond ideas*
> *Of wrongdoing and rightdoing*
> *There is a field.*
> *I'll meet you there*
> *When the soul lies down in that grass*
> *The world is too full to talk about.*
> *Ideas, language, even the phrase 'each other'*
> *Doesn't make any sense."*

My next dream seems to confirm my acceptance of the guidance from 'the writing on the wall.'

Dream: Transformation

I am in a congregation. Sr Kathleen is in front conducting and singing, "The beauty of Christ is all around me, and the beauty of Christ is within me."

She is fully involved as she sways and sings effortlessly and in harmony as she conducts us, a congregation that now seems to have become an orchestra.

Reflection: That such transformation, a congregation becoming an orchestra, is possible, seems amazing. An orchestra allows every instrument to be heard. It indicates the intricate harmony that comes from allowing every instrument to be individually expressed. When we work with diversity, represented by the congregation, and use Christ's teachings, we can aspire to the harmony enjoyed by a musical ensemble in perfect accord.

******

We have been looking at the principle of polarity in dreams, now we turn to unity and the role of dreams in our spiritual growth and development of consciousness. We are constantly faced with new challenges. Having once fought to individuate ourselves from our parents we must make our peace with their mortality and our own. The wisdom of dreams, as we see in the next two chapters, fortifies us for that journey.

Chapter Eleven

By My Heart I Knew

The sparrows were brighter than peacocks here
And their dogs outran our fallow deer
And honeybees had lost their stings
And horses were born with eagles' wings.
Robert Browning, *The Pied Piper of Hamelin*

'Twas but a dream, yet by my heart I knew,
Which still was panting, part of it was true.
Aphra Behn, *The Dream*

Sometimes we have long and complicated dreams that exhaust us in the dreaming, not to mention having to write them down and then contemplate them. The labour involved can seem like too much trouble. It can be easier to simply dismiss them as 'yet another crazy dream.' Other dreams can be so short that we might equally be tempted to dismiss them, thinking of them as 'tiny snippets,' unworthy of investigation. *Every* dream has something to offer. It is always worthwhile to be respectful to what has been brought to your attention.

I am reminded again of the story of the widow's mite from the Gospel of Mark. Jesus had been watching the crowd putting their money into the Temple treasury and observed that many rich people put in large amounts, but the poor widow gave all she had. Jesus told His disciples that this meant she had given more than anyone, no matter what the amount given. Our Soul is like this widow, giving us all it has to get through to us. Sometimes it will try in elaborate ways and sometimes in small but hugely significant ways, all in a bid for us to see the purity of intention.

Consider the dream that follows, of which there could be none shorter:

Dream: Calpol

I wake up with the word 'Calpol' in my mind, wondering what it could mean.

Reflection: Not being the mother of young children, I knew this was not simply 'raw material' left over from my previous day. And in keeping with my commitment to be curious and respectful to each and every snippet from the dream world, I became interested in what this tiny dream might have to offer me.

'Calpol' is the brand name of a British paracetamol remedy for the soothing of teething gums. I began to wonder what 'teething problems' I was having in my life at that time. Sure enough, it was not difficult to discover them in relation to a new relationship in my life. The teething metaphor offered me the wise view that this was a time requiring patience and understanding. And, as with the cutting of baby teeth, this time would pass. Later, we would be able to 'get our teeth into the situation.' Friends who happened to be young mothers told me that teething pain starts any time from three months onwards. I was just about three months into the relationship at this time. The honeymoon period was ending and being replaced with the 'teething problems' of necessary development - the evolution from breast milk to solid food.

Here was the wisdom required in the struggle of a fledgling relationship. Patience and understanding were required of me for the reluctant partner who resisted the challenge to 'give up the breast,' so to speak, and develop the teeth that would be required to process the more 'solid food' of life and relationship.

In the dream world, we sometimes experience an immaculate unity between our human and divine natures. Often described as 'out of this world,' this transpersonal singularity is rarely accessible to us in waking life. We feel it as an 'Ah ha!' moment of insight or pure knowing. When divining the wisdom of dreams, I look out for such revelations. When they occur, there is no doubt a message has been delivered from the unconscious realm to consciousness.

Dream: On the Road to Freedom

In a city hospital, there is someone on an IV drip (intravenous intervention). I am looking at her birth certificate and at a picture of her now as an old woman (she resembles a neighbour) weighing only eight stone, with excrement coming from her rectum and blood coming from the IV where it is attached to her hand. I call for a doctor to come quickly. A lovely young male doctor comes, and he remembers that I have already asked him for directions out of this place. He draws out a map for me, telling me that when I get onto this road, it is the one that everyone has to get on to go anywhere, and it is the road to freedom. He gives me the map and calls me sweetheart as he tells me it's over the bridge with the railings at the corner. I know this place, and now as I get out of the city, my father seems to be with me. I am driving now, and it's as if I am taking my father out of hospital with me. The image of the nice doctor stays with me.

Reflection: Three weeks after this dream my father died. I have to admit I am not an urban warrior! For me, the city is necessary to visit at times and my discomfort there resembles what hospital was like for my father. And how perfect a symbol of our life cycle's amplitude is the birth certificate in conjunction with the dying woman. Sometimes we have no more control over our bodies in the end than we had in the beginning. The types of vulnerability are similar, as we find here. The Doctor (representing the healing force) recognises that I have already asked for a way out of this place and gives me direction. This seems to confirm what we all know about life, i.e. that we all have to take this turning point (death) at some time. For me, the turning point was when I realised that to be healed and to contribute to healing was the most important thing in my life. Going over a bridge to find my destination indicates a transition and the bridge's corner location also suggests a new direction.

Around this time, my father himself dreamed that he was having his best suit of clothing cleaned. I knew there was no significant family occasion about to happen, and that there was only one place of importance he was going, Eternity. Not only was his dream preparing him, but by his telling me this, I was also being prepared. Incidentally, when we dream of neighbours, it can sometimes mean that something is in close proximity to us. In this instance, Death was in close proximity.

Without my knowing (at a conscious level) what lay around the corner, my unconscious gave me the following dream a mere ten days before my father died.

Dream: Preparation

A funeral is coming into our home parish church. The funeral is my father's, and yet somehow, he is also going to be present.

I run down from the altar to the front door where a guard of honour is being formed. Before joining, I must first run back to my house and leave behind me anything unnecessary that I am carrying.

Reflection: This dream is preparing me for an imminent event. The casting aside of burdens I understood as an invitation to make my peace with my father, without bearing him grievances or carrying 'baggage' as I took my place in honouring him and his life, and the life he gave me.

Dream: Feed My Lambs

I said some prayers before going to sleep - fear is close - and I dream that I am feeding lambs on both breasts. Someone has tasted the milk and it seems to be flowing without any problem. I think I am even enjoying the experience. As the dream ends, I am trying to get in tune to sing Psalm 23, 'The Lord Is My Shepherd,' or maybe it's 'Glory to Our God.'

Reflection: In John 21:15-17, Jesus instructs Peter, who claims to love Him, to "Feed my lambs" and again, having been told they love Him, He responds, "Feed my sheep." Psalm 23, appearing at the close of the dream, is a beloved song of reassurance, appreciated by the dreamer as I embarked on my vocational departure:

> *"Yahweh is my shepherd, I lack nothing.*
> *In meadows of green grass he lets me lie.*
> *To the waters of repose he leads me;*
> *there he revives my soul.*
> *He guides me by paths of virtue*
> *for the sake of his name.*
> *Though I pass through a gloomy valley,*
> *I fear no harm;*
> *beside me your rod and your staff*
> *are there, to hearten me.*
> *You prepare a table before me*
> *under the eyes of my enemies;*
> *you anoint my head with oil,*
> *my cup brims over.*
> *Ah, how goodness and kindness pursue me,*
> *every day of my life;*
> *my home, the house of Yahweh,*
> *as long as I live!"*

My unconscious was preparing me for the work to come and the leaving behind of regular, reliable work for a way of life centred on healing.

The Religious Significance of Dreams

For me, God uses our dreams to put us in touch with an energy or communication source that otherwise we might overlook. Our dreams present gifts and insights that help us grow and approach our fullest potential. Through dreams, we are encouraged to discover our innate creativity and intuitive powers. How appropriate and wonderful the invitation from our Creator to 'co-create' and involve ourselves more deeply with our life's meaning and purpose! In *Dreams and Spiritual Growth: A Christian Approach to Dreamwork*, Strephon Kaplan-Williams and colleagues write:

"God is trying to get us to bring our anxiety and fear to the surface, so He can fill us with love, peace and trust. God is calling us as individuals, and as a community, to risk confronting the 'nightmares' in our waking lives, as well as our dreams, in order to release in us energies for healing and courage. People who approach dreams with such attitudes as these are certainly very much in tune with some of the best in the Christian theological tradition."

Morton Kelsey, in *Dreams: A Way to Listen to God*, also speaks about coming into a closer relation with the Dreamer within and suggests that this Dreamer is none other than the Holy Spirit, helping us see ourselves as we are and showing us what we can become:

"If one could find this inner Dreamer who speaks in the perennial language of images, we can find fewer better ways than writing down our dreams and then meditating upon them and bringing them before the One who gave them to us. If we would complain that He should speak more clearly, it is helpful to remember that."

About ten weeks after my father's death, I had the following dream.

Dream: Knowing

I am hearing voices from a heavenly place or a spirit plane. I know they are present and I know they can be seen too, though I cannot see them. I am defending myself in the knowledge that there is communication taking place and Dad is here. I know he knows this to be true.

In the next scene, I'm with someone, and we've been given or else just bought t-shirts. The artist has just painted an individual scriptural scene for each of us on the t-shirts. On the front, mine has a beautiful painted scene and the Commandments, as they were written on the stone tablets given to Moses. The scene on the front could have been from a painting of the Road to Emmaus. I look at the woman and ask her if there is anything major in store for me this year. She looks at me with clear eyes and says that I am where I'm meant to be, in the West, without any doubt. She then goes on to tell me other things about myself, and I wonder how she knows. She says I am a shrink.

Reflection: The dream consoled me, showing me that my belief that my father was in the heavenly realm was correct and that I was exactly where I needed to be. Note the pun, when we say, "Been there, done that, bought the T-shirt," we not only have had an experience but also have the evidence. Of course concrete evidence of an experience with the unseen realm and the souls therein is impossible to produce and yet this is exactly what happened on the road to Emmaus, when the disciples had the experience of having walked with their risen Christ.

The strikingly clear eyes represent clear vision, appropriate to a sleeping state in which our Ego has stepped aside and our inner vision is clearest. I wondered where the word 'shrink' (slang for therapist or analyst) fits in, as it is not a term I use. I concluded that Ego needs to shrink for Self to expand.

A further consolation comes from the personal Artist who dwells within us as someone, or a part of us, that has intimate knowledge of us. I believe this to be our Soul/Self, the guiding force that is always on the lookout for our well being on the path of life, as a good parent would.

In the book of Proverbs 3:6 we read: "In every course you take, have him in mind: he will see that your paths are smooth."

******

The next dream came at a time when I was being invited into rural communities to talk about dream wisdom.

Dream: I Will Make You Fishers of Men

A community of people has gathered for a dance. The musicians are local, and as one group leaves, another more local group takes the stage. I am sitting around with family members. We are sitting on the road in a sloped position. It is raining and seems to be getting dark. We move closer to the middle of the road where there are candles lit to warm our hands. It suddenly gets brighter. I am now walking with a couple that represent humility. We are walking through a bog and speaking of old days and old ways as we notice the lazy beds from our days of famine.

As we come out of that scene, we go in a side door to the Chapel of Adoration in Ballintubber Abbey. As we enter, I notice a man from the dance place, and he greets me. The Sacred Host is on display, and I am carrying a gun or fishing rod with a Host on top of it as bait. As I sit down, I notice my business card on the floor. I am not sure if someone has dropped it, or thrown it away, or left it here for advertising. I think to myself, it would be a good place to advertise my work. A woman sits beside me, and it seems the meeting is about dream work.

Reflection: Let's look at the symbols here. The Host represents spiritual nourishment, and for me, this is at the heart of dream work. For a community of people drawn together for celebration and music, dance is the natural outcome and provides a wonderful way of interacting. 'Being known,' as I know well from the traditional

175

county of Mayo where I live, is central to local community, and having a place to come together to worship and celebrate binds the people together. Our dreams provide us with an opportunity to bring our individual inner 'community' together and urge us to nourish and heal our diversities.

Interestingly, this dream draws attention to the lazy beds in the landscape. These undug ridges are permanent reminders of our past history here in Connacht, undug since the potato blight that wiped out their crop and now scarring the landscape as tangible evidence of an earlier wound. In a way, such reminders keep us in touch with where we have come from.

Our dreams also put us in touch, in their case, with wounds and hungers from our own personal history. Often, when we are deeply wounded, we 'let the dust settle' for some time before we can talk about the pain. The danger in such a silence is that we develop a resistance or reluctance to return to the feelings and think we are healed, when in fact, we have merely avoided the painful process of reopening the wound for healing. This is where the power of the gun often replaces the power of love or the healing power of the Eucharist. The gun represents our defensiveness. This defensive approach slows and damages the healing process, which requires openness, humility and vulnerability.

Dream: Development at the Crossroads

A lot of development is happening at the crossroads. As well as the new buildings, four of which are visible, the road is also being worked on.

Reflection: This is a straightforward dream showing the development of the Self. Characteristically, the unconscious uses a pun that is obvious, once we take the time to recognise it. When we describe ourselves as 'being at a crossroads' in life, it means we have choices and decisions to make and here the Psyche is reflecting progress at this point in life.

Dream: Second Bloom

Karen dreams she is given a red lily by a young man of about twenty-two or twenty-three years old.

Reflection: At first, Karen had difficulty in understanding this dream and wondered why the young man and why, a red Lily. I asked her if she knew this flower from anywhere in particular and she then remembered a woman giving her this plant about two years before. More recently, Karen came to realise that the plant was being neglected, and she set about taking care of the lily again. To her surprise and delight, it was now thriving and about to bloom again. On closer examination, she realised that the woman who had given her the lily had been abandoned unexpectedly by her husband and was, only now, reclaiming her beauty and bloom again. This was an exact mirror image for Karen, whose husband had abandoned her two years earlier. She too, was now reclaiming and remembering how she was twenty-two or twenty-three years earlier, when they had first met. The young man was representative of her Animus, or male/thinking side of herself. She realised that she, too, could bloom again, as indeed she has.

The two-year interval was a necessary time of grieving for the unexpected loss. Yet, the part of her, like the plant, that endured neglect during her relationship, still hung in there faithfully for the possibility that life would return and bloom once more. Water was all it took, and again, knowing that water is symbolic of our emotional world, Karen, too, had needed to shed the water of tears in her emotional struggle to come to terms with her loss, betrayal and grief. This step taken, she could bloom again.

Dream: A Huge Project

A very big site is being developed. At first, the whole scene seems to be in chaos, but the developer seems to know what he is doing and points out to me the section that is already in place, such as the pipes, which represent the water works. Then he points out to me where there is going to be a house at the centre. The site is typical of a building site, with cement, etc., everywhere. The builder now shows me where the part that was old, shaky and unsafe has now been made safe and firmer. One half has been taken away (it was an old school), and is no longer required. A man is working with a drill as he breaks new ground, and he seems to know what he has to do.

Reflection: This huge project, or new development, speaks volumes to me, the dreamer. When I speak 'as the dream,' using Fritz Perls' Gestalt approach, I quickly realise that the task being undertaken is the latest challenge in my own self-development. I am happy to discover that the developer seems to know what he is doing! The Developer of such a big project can be none other than the Lord of my life. He points out to me that although I am unable to grasp fully what He is working on, He can show me the work that is already in place.

Pipes, containing waters' inflow and outflow, are a good example of the emotional world being worked on (water is well-known as a symbol of the emotional realm). The removal of the 'old school' (a phrase denoting an old way of thinking), useful in the past but no longer required, is a very encouraging element. Pipes, by contrast, are a necessary part of any inhabited structure, vital to install before later stages of development. This symbol also supports the need to have emotional structures in place for a child before they are expected to build their higher levels of understanding. Note also, the language - the old, shaky and unsafe has been made safe and firm.

The most significant part of this dream, appropriately for a dream about property, is the location. All this development is being built *around a house*. Remember Jung's notion of the house being the Self? Here I discover the potential of my own development being singled out and worked with. When speaking in Gestalt as the workman using the drill, I said, "This is a difficult part that has to be broken through, but I must stick to it as it is all necessary and part of the work that has to be done."

I had this dream in 1994, as the first seeds of this book were being planted, and in order to continue the difficult task involved, I had to remove the 'old school of thinking' full of messages from my negative Animus, telling me I could not do this. Thankfully, I was able to trust the essential message of the dream, in which not only the Developer but also his workman seemed to know what had to be done and what they were doing. The 'worker' in me knows too what I have to do, and at this stage, it feels as if the 'drill' was necessary to break the tough surface of resistance in pursuit of progress. Messy and slow though it may be, this dream is a source of encouragement.

******

A particular poem by WB Yeats captures both my own vulnerability (in putting this book, one of my life's dreams, out into the world) and the spiritual essence of this book itself, in which I too wish for the 'Cloths of Heaven.' It concludes, 'Tread softly because you tread on my dreams.'

As Irish writer and poet Ed Boyne said, "There is no greater mystic or interpreter of the dream life than WB Yeats."

******

Dream: Ready for a New Teacher

A woman is talking about her relationship to a non-existent sister of her friend. She says she is ready for a new teacher. The dreamer understands what she is saying and responds by saying that each relationship has something to teach us about ourselves. The dreamer is in the same bed as the woman she is talking to.

Reflection: Getting into bed with someone can imply close connections, merging ideas or getting close to another's quality in oneself. When we dream about someone who does not exist, it can be an opportunity to look at what is *not* in our actual life and an encouragement for us to be creative in filling that absence.

Dream: Inner Child Work

In Miriam's dream, her father is after making the fire, and she notices a small child is messing with tablets (pills), and yet, she is not conscious of the danger. Suddenly she realises he has swallowed some. They are her father's tablets. She takes the child outside and puts her fingers in his throat to make him throw up. He vomits up two different tablets - one long, white one with the word 'toxic' written on it and another round one.

Reflection: Miriam was doing some work on herself regarding her father's character in her behaviour. When she realises the danger to the child she 'takes him outside,' suggesting he had been inside. This connected her to the inner-child work she was doing in her therapy and helped her to spew out that which was toxic of her father's fire/anger when she was a child. She became aware of what she had swallowed of his thinking (the male child) when she was young. She is now taking the child into her own care and instinctively knows what to do once she becomes aware.

******

The following letter/testimony came from a young woman, Caroline, at the end of her psychotherapy process. She acknowledges her fears as she entered into the exciting/scary process of psychotherapy. We worked with the wisdom of her dreams during the journey.

Dear Kathleen
I can't just start to write it down - I want to introduce it. I don't know why it has taken so long to write this dream down and give it away.

It was not that I didn't want to! I was just never ready to cross the threshold before now. I think that's why it's fitting in here at this transition - leaving (therapy). I have to cross another threshold - one that frightens and excites me both at the same time. That feeling reminds me of one of the moments that inspired my dream, perhaps that is why it fits here.

Dream: My Dream - Our Journey

I dreamt my partner and I were having a baby together. We were both so excited. I was in the hospital with my feet in stirrups and wearing the hospital gown. My partner was holding my hand and we were both delighted about what was happening. My waters broke - but the fluid that came out was blood and it was a vibrant red colour. It wasn't clear as in water.

I could see my pregnant belly bare before me and my legs spread as I pushed with all my might and squeezed my partner's hand. I gave birth to a little girl called 'Willomeena.'

She had jet-black hair, and her little red face was all scrunched up and crying as my partner showed her to me before I took her myself. When I held her, I was so proud of her and so in love with her. I was so amazed that we had made this perfect little being together, and I loved her with all my heart.

Caroline's Reflection: I explored this dream later in my therapy with Kathleen. It was early in my process with her. We explored where I might have known the name 'Willomeena' from. I couldn't remember knowing anyone with that name, either in real life or from fiction. After a while Kathleen asked me if I knew a 'Will' or a 'Meena.' I did. When I explored my memories, I knew both a 'Will' and a 'Meena' and they were both part of experiences I had in my life where I gained new levels of maturity and independence as a woman and as a person.

When I was twenty, I went to study in America for a year. It was to be my longest time away from home and my first time to live out of my home country. The fear I had was that if things went poorly for me or were hard for me over there, I would be on my own and would have to figure things out on my own, without being able to run home to Mammy! I was also excited about what this adventure would bring me.

On the way to the airport, I held Mammy's hand the whole way and I was rigid with nerves at the thought of walking away and saying goodbye to my parents. There were two young men at the airport who were also going to America to study for the year and who were on the same programme as I was, one of whom was called 'Will.' I struggled with my goodbye to my parents and had to break away when Will stretched out his arm and embraced me in a hug. He told my parents not to worry that he would look after me. In that simple gesture, he comforted both my parents and me and made it easier for them to let me go and for me to walk away towards my own independence.

I looked after myself that year and became more confident and more independent than ever before. I actually don't think I have yet equalled that year in terms of what I gained from it in self-confidence.

'Meena' was the name of a psychologist I met shortly after my undergraduate degree in psychology. My mum introduced her to me, and she agreed to meet with me to offer any career advice that might help as I tried to figure out where to go next in my life. I thought she would just meet me as my mother's daughter, but she didn't - she met me as me, Caroline - worthy of time and capable of anything. I felt like a real professional and not a child in grown-up shoes.

I met both of these people at times of transition in my life - times where I became 'me' and 'myself,' an independent person and a professional in my own right.

Kathleen and I looked at the possible meaning behind my waters breaking and blood flowing instead of clear liquid. Menstruation was what came to mind. Menstruation and birth in the same scene brought us to wonder about what I had given birth to in myself that my dream was trying to show me through 'Willomeena'!

The onset of menstruation marks the transition from adolescence to womanhood. 'Willomeena' was casting up memories of times where I had transitioned into a more mature and independent young woman. Was this what I had given birth to? My own beautiful independent femininity! She was co-created with my partner in my dream. How fitting was this? My poor and suffering partner, who by the very fact that I love him so greatly, triggers so many of my childhood wounds, and with whom I have so often acted like a very small child and expected the type of love, commitment, tolerance and understanding from him that a three-year-old would demand from a mother!

In my relationship with him, my inner child came forth demanding attention and care. If I could only give it, then or now, what a strong and independent woman I could become. But give it to myself I must, not demand it from my now husband. This was my challenge - to nurture my baby, 'Willomeena.' She had the potential to be so great, as shown to me by the associations she had cast up by her name, which had already pointed me in the direction of my potential.

Three years on and just as the toddler says so fiercely, "My do it myself," as she experiments with her struggle for independence, I too, have decided to do it for myself for a while and will leave the nurturing bosom of my therapy space. The question is, have I internalised mother (therapist) and can I hold her with me as I move out into the world on my own? I certainly can plagiarise some of her (Kathleen) expressions and phrases!

Recently I had an inspiring dream, which seems to confirm my readiness. Firstly, I need to set the scene.

During my process, almost every time I explored a powerful childhood memory where I could see myself as the child bereft of understanding or acceptance, Kathleen would always instruct me, "Tell her you understand. Tell her you see her. Put the little child on your knee and give her what she needs now." This guidance was to be done in the realm of inner visualisation.

"I can't" were the words I responded with, while I fumed and resented the fact/fear that this would never work for me. I couldn't put 'little Caroline' on my knee - it made no difference - or so I thought!

I had recently done some family constellations work based on the work of the German psychotherapist, Bert Hellinger, which Kathleen had recommended to me many times during our process. In this work, I had explored an ancestral issue relating to years of unresolved hurt and anger on my maternal grandmother's side. The root of the anger seemed to have begun with my great-grandmother and was passed down through my grandmother.

In my dream the two women who embodied the roles of these women during my family constellation work were present. My great-grandmother had a stronger presence. She was taking me to the train station in Dublin, where I was to get a train home.

During our exploration of this seemingly short dream, Kathleen asked me about my most recent experience of being on this train. The scene was familiar, as I had only recently been on this train from Dublin. I was supporting a colleague who was facilitating the move of a foster child to visit her birth parents. The child was only just over four years old and this was her first time to meet me. I knew she was finding the experience stressful.

On the return journey, she was tired, uncomfortable and couldn't sleep. I had already noticed she was a little more agitated in her body and finding it difficult to sit still. I debated internally and eventually asked her if she would like to sit on my knees. (I didn't think she would want to, or that it would make any difference as I wasn't either of her two mammies.) But she did sit on my knee, and it did make a difference! She cuddled in and fell asleep.

The next week, as we made the same journey to re-visit the child's birth parents she sat on my knee again, cuddled up and fell asleep for most of the journey, there and back.

I was informed that she was coping better with the transition and separation from this point on. I cannot say whether this had anything to do with me, but I certainly believe the nurture and warmth helped. How interesting it was for me that *my great-grandmother was delivering me to this destination!*

In the dream my great-grandmother also took me to her flat, which, when I looked at it in therapy, actually was more like my paternal grandmother's house. Only one day previously, I had been there with my family. We were talking about an issue where I felt I had been treated unfairly, and the more I pressed the issue, the more dismissive they became. Then I became petty and childish, as I felt so angry at how they treated me.

I ended up feeling even worse and less understood or accepted. "Little Caroline was angry and needed attention now from the adult Caroline," as Kathleen would say! I didn't nurture little Caroline that day. I tried to force others to understand me. This is a pattern I have discovered (through my therapy) that often plays out with my partner, to no success.

My dream was showing me something very important. My great-grandmother symbolised recent work I had done on the power of ancestral anger. She took me first to a place where I had recently been very angry with my family, where 'little Caroline' needed, but did not get, my adult understanding as I focused on getting others to understand and meet my needs instead, thinking my own understanding was/is not enough.

My great-grandmother then took me to a scene where my understanding was enough and did make a difference. Neither of this child's (mammies) mothers was there to hold her on that train journey when she needed it, but I was. I was able to hold her on my knee and understand her...

And she felt better. I held her for as long as she needed. I held her on my knee and saw her needs...

And it did make a difference - just like Kathleen had always told me to do with my own inner child - my 'little' Caroline. To do this means I can free myself from trying to make others, especially my partner, do it for me, when really the only one who can do it is me anyway. Had I internalised mother (therapist)? It looks like it!

Is 'Willomeena,' now three-years-old, ready to take her first steps as an independent little being? She was first created through my relationship with my partner and introduced through my relationship with Kathleen. As 'Willomeena' takes her first steps will I, Caroline, no longer feel, "I can't" when I need to hold 'little' Caroline on my knees?

My dreams tell me I have already learned that it works. Now I just need to do it for myself!

Kathleen's Reflection: My Dream - Our Journey
I do not need to elaborate much on the above transcript as Caroline has already reflected on the significance of her dream. I would just like to draw attention to the fact that Will and Meena are male and female, and here we see the wise use of the dream wisdom in using not only names, but gender too, to get a point of importance across. For Caroline it was important to have both her male (logos) and female (emotional) side engaged in supporting her in her transition.

Dream: Ripe Fruit

I am going to someone's house and have only a red apple to offer them. I'm thinking it is not very much, as normally I would have wine to bring. As I wake up, I am recognising the apple as the 'fruit of the tree of knowledge' which caused Adam and Eve to open their eyes to a new reality.

Reflection: To 'open our eyes' or 'wake up' is like coming out of our unconscious state and into consciousness, and with this new consciousness comes responsibility for the consequences of our actions. It is time, according to this dream, for me to put value on what I have to offer to others. The fact that the apple is red and not green seems to suggest ripeness.

When Eve first opened her eyes in the Garden of Eden as a result of eating the forbidden fruit, she didn't just enjoy the spectacular vision. She nudged and/or persuaded Adam to open his eyes too. And what a price she paid for that awakening! To be cast out of the bliss of ignorance and into the knowledge of consciousness.

In Ireland, it is customary when visiting someone to bring some gift or contribution in anticipation and acknowledgment of the hospitality about to be received. It is also a familiar belief that no child comes into the world without some gift.

We each must undertake the task of finding out what this gift is and bring it to fruition.

In the next dream, I am also being challenged to walk in faith as I invite the dream group to speak as willing leaders.

Dream: Isaiah Reads Moses

I am leading a dream group. The prophet Isaiah is reading about Moses. I invite this woman to speak as Moses from her dream. I invite the dreamer to bring the dream alive by giving the various parts a voice in the here and now, thus owning the energy of the symbol.

Reflection: We know from Scripture that Moses was called to be a leader and he led his people through the wilderness, in faith, into the promised 'land of milk and honey.' When we think about the 'Moses part' in all of us, we are reminded of the struggles with faith, trust, hope, hunger, patience, purpose and promise. Isaiah in the dream above is vague, yet present, and when I think of Isaiah, I think of promise. My favourite passage comes from Isaiah 49:15 where God promises He will never forget us, "Does a woman forget her baby at the breast, or fail to cherish the son of her womb? Yet even if these forget, I will never forget you."

There must have been so much that was unclear for Moses, yet he continued to obey and trust as he led his people in the wilderness. This dream encourages and challenges me to continue to move forward in trust in my field of dream wisdom. *(See Guidance Dream on page 120.)*

Dream: Discipline

A film is being shown, and we're watching it when suddenly I am involved in the actual movie. There is a general inspection (the task of the army) taking place. I notice everyone has to march, even the children, and everyone is asked to make some garment. One guy is disfigured and he must make a garment in accordance with his shape. Now he is the one being called forth by number to come and demonstrate. He has to climb up a very difficult ladder. I am now being called to do this.

As I climb the ladder, I know the position is being shifted or changed, making it more difficult or almost impossible, but I still try and am nearly at the top when I beg for a helping hand to pull me up. As I look down I can see where the ladder was first placed and should have been held in place but wasn't.

Now, I know I am being filmed in the movie at this point and I come running back through the field with a book in my hand. In the dream I know the name of the book as I arrive on our street at home. Now,

I realise I have lost most of the book and only have a few pages in my hand. I turn to go back to where I have come from in order to find what I have lost, but first I have to get past Maria, who is trying to turn or park her car on the narrow width of our street. I manage to squeeze past her, and she gets out of her car and we talk. I now understand why she is being unfriendly but it is okay as we chat and I tell her about having to go back to find the book that I have lost. She talks to me about all the visitors I have and hopes they will be fewer.

Reflection: Mindful of the importance of opening scenes where dreams are concerned, I notice the immediate change in role from observing to participating. We are meant to be participants in our lives, and watching the movies gives us an opportunity to see how others do it, and how we might identify with different characters or project aspects of ourselves onto them. Watching the action on stage or screen is another way of having an objective look at ourselves. Only when we stand back from a situation can we see more clearly what is happening and gain insight into what needs to be achieved.

The next stage of the dream shows inspection and contribution. When I think of the army, I think of discipline, and here, even the children are asked to contribute and be creative in accordance with their ability or disability (the disfigured person). The dream focuses on some distortion, and as artists from Michelangelo to Picasso have known, out of distortion often comes our greatest creativity. The disfigured one is the one called forth to demonstrate his willingness to undertake a difficult task.

'Climbing the ladder' is often used as a metaphor for achievement or success and can also be described as moving to a higher position through taking one step at a time. Again the words of Scripture (Ps. 118:22) come to mind where we are told that, "It was the stone rejected by the builders that proved to be the keystone." The reference is to Jesus Himself.

Gestalt, we remember, is the approach used to bring a symbol to life by giving it a voice in the here-and-now. Sometimes it seems to me that this idea is but another way of trying to do what Jesus was doing. Using an image to represent the Self and giving rejected parts a value and a voice is akin to Jesus saying he was the 'door or the 'lamb' or the 'bread.' One of the important things to note about this dream is my willingness to try a difficult task, difficult to the point of impossibility. This is where I beg for help to get me through.

Again, turning to Scripture, Jesus undertook a major task willingly, and when He was almost there, He too cried out for help, "Father, if you are willing, take this cup away from me." (Luke 22:42) The book I run back with could be the 'Book of Life' or maybe this book that you are holding now. It could be, that all those years ago, I was being offered a glimpse of the struggle to come!

As the dream states, I have to go back through the fields I have come from to find the missing pages. At this moment, I feel as if I am in that dream as I go back and sift through the many books of dream journals I have recorded over the years. *The Field of Dreams* could be an appropriate title but before I get carried away, I must first squeeze past Maria, who is trying to turn and/or park her car on the narrow width of our street. To turn a car on a narrow street takes many manoeuvres and sometimes, with patience, we just manage to do it. (This was my hope with this book, which I was not confident of writing at the outset.) Maria represented someone who had succeeded in achieving what I had only imagined or dreamed of. I took her unfriendly or non-accepting attitude towards me in the dream to be a chastisement for the many visitors I was entertaining, instead of being more disciplined in order to achieve what I must do, and then her advice is never too late. To quote Ephesians 3:20:

"Glory be to him whose power, working in us, can do infinitely more than we can ask or imagine."

Chapter Twelve

Between Two Worlds – Idir Eatarthu

During the day, our souls gather their...impression of us...our
Spirits collect these impressions, keep them together, like wisps of
smoke in a bag, then, when we're asleep, our brains open up these
bags of smoke... and take a look...
Marsha Norman, *The Fortune Teller*

You see things and you say, "Why?"
But I dream things that never were; and I say, "Why not?"
George Bernard Shaw, *Back to Methuselah*

About a week prior to my mother's death, she had a dream which she shared with my sister-in-law. In the dream, she was getting married again and said something about the fact that I was attending to her. Hearing this, I figured that she was indeed about to be united again with my father, who had died twelve years earlier. If being united is what marriage is about, this time their marriage was to be in the Eternal World. This dream of my mother's helped me during the final two weeks of her earthly existence. I could accept that her destiny was already orchestrated by her Soul.

During these two weeks, while she seemed to hover between two worlds as a result of a stroke, I dreamed that my sisters and I were getting ready to be bridesmaids. We all wore variations of black clothing. As it is customary to wear black in the event of death and mourning, I was clearly 'getting ready' to assist my mother in her passage from this life to the next and so it came to pass.

Our dreams are like messengers between the unseen world, or world of Spirit, and this world of Matter with which we are more identified.

Freud felt that most dreams are based on unmet needs or the idea of wish fulfilment. I believe the following experience confirms that they come from a more objective place than our suppressed needs, whilst still respecting those needs and bringing them to consciousness.

My mother's lifelong friend died suddenly, less than two years before my mother. Her daughter, Jane, told me she had had, since her death, many visits from her mother in her dreams. After each 'dream visit' Jane felt again the acute loss of her mother and continued to mourn her. During one of those dreams, Jane told her mother about the strong sense of her presence she felt after each dream and wondered if her visits were 'actual' in her dreams or if they were 'just her dreams.'

Then Jane had this dream.

Dream: Forewarning

I am standing in the same place where I was when I received the phone call which told me of my mother's death. Now, I see my mother with her lifelong friend, Kathleen's mother. Now, standing at this spot are Kathleen and her sisters and family members gathered in prayer as the tide comes in around them.

Reflection: One week *after* Jane had this dream, my mother suffered a stroke. She died two weeks later. Through the dream, it was as if Jane's mother, from her new domain in the Spirit world, was able to see and forewarn Jane that this is how she would know that her visits were indeed real *and* that she could foresee events. The statement could be understood as saying that my own family are now in the same place that Jane was when she got the news that her mother had died.

Why else would Jane's dream have chosen the same place? Her mother was showing her that soon my sisters and I would be in the same emotional place in which Jane and her sisters had been when they suffered their loss. The tide coming in again seems to suggest the law of nature, or the emotional ebb and flow of life.

******

Dream: Emotional Crossroads

We are laying our mother to rest in her grave at a crossroads. I am aware that her grave is on the side of the crossroads that leads to Aughagower graveyard where she is actually laid to rest. The other side of the crossroads led to her earthly home in Lanmore. I notice that the tide is coming in as her coffin is being lowered and I suddenly can see through it and the tidal water and I notice she is opening her eyes and speaking. The scene now shifts back to her hospital bed where she is telling us she saw and heard everything, and it was as if she was saying "Thank you."

Reflection: I always look at where the dream is taking place, knowing there is always a reason behind the setting. If we take it that water represents emotions, and look at the graphic image of this dream, it is easy to recognise the statement. Emotions are like the tide, coming in unpredictable waves.

There are four directions at a typical crossroads. I find it interesting that this dream has my mother being laid to rest on the side that leads to her final resting place and not on the side that leads to her home.

Within two weeks, and on the eve of a gathering to visit Mother's grave, my sister had the following dream.

Dream: Higher Level

My sister, Jo, sees Mother at home amongst us as we gather there in her memory and honour. She is seated at a higher level, as if at a higher counter, and as my sister reaches out to greet her and ask if everything is all right, she calls her by name and says everything is fine. Jo, knowing she is dead, then asks her enthusiastically whom she had first met on the other side. Mother names her recently departed brother and continues to name many others, but Jo, in her eagerness to know if she had met her beloved, interrupts her and asks if she had met Dad yet. "Yes," she says, "he is fine and has gained four stone in weight."

Reflection: My mother's position at a higher level is significant, confirming the belief that our soul moves to higher levels after it leaves the body. Her husband's weight gain seems to confirm Mother's idea of being taken care of, as she spent most of their married life trying to nurture my father with food. For my mother, putting on weight meant 'thriving.'

******

One final dream which reassured me during these weeks after mother's death was as follows.

Dream: Going Back Home

*In this dream I am in a gathering with family and friends outside my mother's recently departed home waiting for her to come and be with us as we came together in her memory. She drives up the road and does not stop or become distracted by our presence. She simply continues her journey up the road. When I go after her she tells me she must **go back home to where she came from**.*

Reflection: I was comforted to recognise the message in this dream. In her earthly existence she so often made the journey up that same road going **back home,** as she used to say, to her own childhood home from where she had come. The difference in the dream scene is where she is now driving a car suggesting she is now in a more empowered vehicle than when she cycled there. It was good to realise she was not trapped here in this realm and although she was very attached to her home and family here she was making a clear statement that it was now time to go back to her **heavenly home from where she had originally come**.

******

My friend, Maureen Huntley, a renowned Holistic Nutritional Counsellor in the United States, shared a particularly relevant dream.

Dream: The Glass Elevator

Mom and I are in an elevator. It is glass. The building is glass, translucent, and I can see everything as though it's a prism. I look down at Mom, who is in a wheelchair. (She was never in one up to now in life.) The elevator is going up and up and, as it does, I see an atrium which is all glass - big, beautiful, clear. The elevator stops at the top floor. The doors open. I push the wheelchair out and head out into this atrium, in awe of its majesty.

As we move along, I notice a huge boardroom, again clear and see-through. As we get closer, I can see that it has a round table with twelve seats. I open the door and push Mom in. Looking up, I see that the seats are all taken, except one, the one that we are in front of. Mom leans forward and puts her hand on the back of the chair and starts to pull it out. I look to her right and see that it is her brother John. He was next to her in age, but he's deceased. I look around and see that all the seats are occupied by her eleven siblings. They are all deceased. I feel panicked. I realise that they want her with them.

I look back at John and I say to him, "No! No, not now!" He looks at me, confused. I put my hand on my mother's hand to stop her moving the chair back. She is now standing. I look to our left and I see her sister, Martha. She was her big sister, protector, her friend.

Martha was a second mother to me. "No!" I look at her and say. "Please, not now. I'm not ready to lose her." "Soon," Martha replies. "Please, give me two more years with her, please!" "OK, but soon."

I push the chair back in and pry Mom's hand off the back. Mom steps back to sit in the wheelchair but I say, "No! Walk, you must walk." We leave, heading back to the elevator. Mom keeps looking back and I keep pulling her forward.

Maureen added a remarkable note to this transcript: "The next day, my father called me at eight in the morning to tell me that my mother had had a massive heart attack during the night. I flew from New Jersey to Chicago to arrive at the hospital by late afternoon. I was a wreck. I ran to her room and when she saw me my mother said, 'Maureen, I thought I was a goner, but there you were!' My Mom passed away peacefully almost two years later. The week before she died, I dreamed again of her passing. In the dream she told me she was tired and done. I told her it was okay."

******

The next dream was notable for the rich mix of sources, woven together expertly to form an arresting sequence of scenes.

Dream: The High Road, Lady Augusta and the Video

Fiona is on a road or path following someone that looks Indian. The path has two levels, and she follows the dark-haired woman on the higher path. At some point, Fiona turns back and sees animals that seem to be in chains, being driven by male and female figures in colourful dress that looks like Scottish kilts. Though the cattle are tied, they are being protected and are somehow in order. When she arrives at her destination, Fiona is shown to her room. She is about to use the telephone to call the number 108 when she doubts that the number is correct. Fiona goes to use the telephone directory to find the number, but drops the directory and it slides down a chute to the basement. She goes down the stairs to find it and there she is introduced by one of the herdsmen to Lady Augusta who owns the house. Lady Augusta takes her to where the directory is and shows her a beautiful playroom equipped with all sorts of toys in action. The scene now changes, and Fiona is being shown a video of herself in lotus position at the edge of the sea while the water washes over her. As the video continues, she is noticing that it is all about her life, and she wonders how these apparent strangers have this coverage of her life. Then Fiona notices her lover is being thrown into a container. She is upset and wants to know what is happening. Then she wakes up.

Reflection: When we explored Fiona's association with these dream images, she felt that India (for her) represented a quest for spirituality. It was now my task to explore with the dreamer the source of this association. Fiona had just returned from a week of Tantric yoga in France, where she had been exposed to the healing powers of the *japa mala*. In India, and other oriental cultures, *mala* means 'garland of flowers' and is used, like the Catholic rosary, for praying or meditating. Usually a *mala* is composed of 108 beads of semi-precious stones, or other materials, united in a single continuous thread. At the end of the *mala*, there is the *guru* bead, a bigger stone or a silver or gold pendant, and the traditional silk tassel, which symbolises the higher chakra, called 'the thousand petals lotus.' The *mala* is a sacred and healing tool which uses numerology, stones and the symbolic *guru* bead and tassel. Every *mala* is unique and created to take care of ourselves on the path of growth and self healing. We can see where the Dream Self got the images used to send her a message.

In the opening scene, we see Fiona choosing to follow the spiritual path, the 'higher road.' At this point, I asked her to tell me about her association with the cattle and the herding folk on the lower road. Why were they wearing kilts? At first, she had no idea but, when I explored further, she said they seemed happy, as if singing along. Naturally I thought of Scotland but said nothing directly, since it is important to let the dreamer come to their own conclusions, while being guided somewhat by highlighting information the dream provided. Thus, I reminded her of the atmosphere in this part of the dream, as well as the colourful dress, and suggested the Scottish song called 'The Bonnie Banks o' Loch Lomond':

"You'll take the high road
And I'll take the low road
And I'll be in Scotland before you..."

This seems like a happy vibrant song and the dream mirrors this energy, yet, when we listen to the words of the song, we find lovers that will never meet again.

The song turns out to be about two men in a Scottish Highlands' jail, one of whom is being released while the other has been sentenced to death. The doomed one tells his comrade that he is taking 'the high road,' meaning the spiritual path, and believes therefore he will be in Scotland or 'Home before the other.' Even though Fiona at first did not make this connection, it is important to be interested in the reason the Dream Self had for choosing this image.

When I enquired about what kind of container her lover was put into, Fiona said it was more like a skip (sometimes called a dumpster). At first her conscious mind was not aware from where she got this image. Then she remembered a skip used on the campus where she had taken her yoga course. On further investigation, we discovered that this skip was used for waste food. I asked Fiona what she felt as she put her waste food into this container. She said she felt it was such a waste – all this perfectly good food being dumped, instead of giving extra portions to the participants at mealtime. When I asked her why, she connected the situation with the systematic thinking of the Germans running the course, who felt that rules must be strictly followed. Fiona had challenged them about the wasteful consequences of their approach, but finally realised she was wasting her energy. The 'system' insisted that each participant got one helping of food at meal times with the remainder simply dumped in this skip. (You could compare the skip to a bowel, since both have an important function in their respective systems, as have our gut feelings when we take heed.)

Taking it that food is energy for the body, I now asked Fiona what other energy she might have been wasting at this time in her life. She quickly realised that she was wasting her energy on a lover. She had talked to an Indian woman about this situation, a conversation which had resulted in an emotional release. Following this, she was more ready to let him go and she chose to follow her spiritual path. The dream used the Indian woman's influence to connect her with the actual experience of that healing.

We now explored why the dream used Animals. It seems that the Animal instinct, or Animal energy, represents the sexual energy symbolised by the base *chakra*. This was an important part of this relationship, but yet insufficiently significant to make it as meaningful as she desired. The dream shows the contentment in the herding folk. This mirrored the contentment in the Scottish song. The doomed man of Loch Lomond was able to accept the fact that he would never see his lover again. His way of coping was to choose the 'higher road' or spiritual path.

The dream therefore, when understood, helped Fiona to celebrate her ability to let her lover go, knowing that her spiritual journey had become more important to her. The video scenes from the basement of the house seem to suggest that in the unconscious part of our Psyche, there is a place where we are truly known, and when we choose to find what we have lost, we can be shown what we need to see in order to continue on our path towards wholeness. This woman is watching herself in the Lotus position. This confirms her commitment to yoga studies.

The waters washing over her make another statement. We are familiar, from emotional dilemmas, with the expression "Let it wash over you" as a way of suggesting surrender and acceptance. Fiona was initially upset about the fact that her lover was only interested in the sexual side of their relationship and did not seem interested in her spiritual quest. This is reflected in the emotion at the end of her dream. The dream also uses the image of the *mala* in using the number 108. The telephone has a similar function to the rosary beads or *mala*, insofar as it helps us to focus and connects us to another dimension.

Even though the insight from this dream was helpful and affirming for Fiona, it was not enough. She was now challenged and supported, as we all are by our dreams, to put this wisdom into *practice*. Fiona did this by developing her new way of living and much work and discipline were required as she parted with her lover (as did Lady Augusta and Prince Augustus of old) and took, in the form of yoga teaching, the spiritual path for home and Self.

******

Like Fiona, I was also challenged at this time, in my case to work at my faith as the church/structure of my own beliefs underwent reconstruction. The Church, in my view, is meant to be a living community of believers rather than being limited to the physical structure or building. In the following dream, I was faced with the question of the Church's real purpose. Was it, as a structure of support, serving or being served by its members?

Dream: Power Goes Out of Church

I am at Mass when suddenly the power goes off. It's as if we all leave the church to go to the toilet. At first, we have to find proper outdoor footwear, and we are in a queue as a trailer of various shoes is being tipped up. I am thinking it will take forever to find mine amongst so many and varied shoes. I then realise I am fine in the shoes I am wearing and leave the scene. Next, I am back at home making dinner for a large gathering of people. The place is in a mess, with fish and liver, and I notice that after everyone has eaten there are scraps all over the floor.

Reflection: The failed power seems to reflect the kind of energy that the Church seemed to be losing at the time of this dream, in the late Eighties. By contrast, the dream image of going to the toilet can be about letting go of something that is no longer good to hold inside. It is also something private and personal, and in this dream the time seems ripe for the private and personal to emerge. At this time, some intimate details were beginning to be brought out into the open about abuses of Church power. Without proper elimination of what is taken in, a body, as well as an institution, will become toxic.

Many people at this time were beginning to express themselves and find healing in ways other than through the Church, going into therapy for healing instead of making confession. Interestingly, the two have very similar functions, offering the seeker of peace an opportunity to reveal their struggles in the presence of a non-judgemental Other. In the experience of such acceptance, grace enters into the participants, allowing healing to take place.

The closing scene of the dream brings to mind the Biblical parable of the loaves and fishes in which scraps were left over after everyone had eaten. In this gathering, Jesus was asking people to do something that at first seemed impossible, and yet, when they did what was commanded of them *in faith*, they were amazed at what proved to be possible.

When I applied the essence of this dream to my own life events, I saw that my new psychotherapeutic vocation was calling me, in another way, to 'feed the people.' The liver is vital in filtering and processing what we ingest before eliminating what is no longer useful. This symbol could also describe the process of psychotherapy, whereby we are required to filter and process all we have taken (and 'been taken in by'!) in our lives. The process requires us to eliminate old beliefs and behaviours that no longer serve us as we find the courage to open up to our more authentic selves and let go of conditional behaviour.

You could say that this is also what Jesus was asking of His followers. When He told them to sit the people down and feed them from five loaves and two fish, they said, "But how can we do this?" Still, they began and discovered that, as they obeyed him, the miracle unfolded.

On the day when I said 'yes' to my training, I had no idea how I was going to fund this expensive education or find room in my life to meet this commitment. I prayed for inspiration and opened the Scriptures to the two following promises, each of which has subsequently been fulfilled for me: "In return my God will fulfil all your needs, in Christ Jesus, as lavishly as only God can." Philippians 4:19.

"Set your hearts on his kingdom first, and on his righteousness, and all these things will be given to you as well. So do not worry about tomorrow; tomorrow will take care of itself. Each day has enough trouble of its own." Matthew 6:33-34.

Shortly after this reassurance, I had the following dream.

Dream: Outer Image versus Inner Work

My parents are painting a large building that they have bought. They are using the colours cream and coral. The front of the building has lovely detail and the walls are very decorative. I suggest that mother leaves the fancy work as it is and just paints the boundary coral. She says she has a golden colour for the designs. I then ask them what they plan to do with it. Mother says we would never have to work again as this place would be let or rented in flats. Now, it is as if I am driving up to where they are, and my godmother is chatting to them. I have the feeling now that they expect me to do this painting, when the scene changes and curtains are being drawn back. I go inside. It is dark and I look around for lights. I eventually find light switches, four or five are in at the side of an old fireplace and covered over with whitewash.

When I put the lights on, I realise the place is in need of a lot of work. As I begin to clean it up, I discover a cupboard full of bread, and beside it my green book called 'Heal My Heart, O Lord.' I am giving bread to whoever is with me to take home with them and am amazed to find so much of all sorts of bread for me to distribute.

Reflection: My first impression draws on another Scriptural quotation, "You who clean the outside of cup and dish and leave the inside full of extortion and intemperance." (Matt. 23:25) Detailing the outside while the inside goes neglected is like 'keeping up appearances' or presenting a persona to the public (the work of an unchecked ego) while not attending to necessary spiritual work. It looks as if I am getting involved in the painting work through feeling guilty. In other words, I am about to live up to my parents' expectations instead of following my own purpose when my godmother appears and the scene changes.

As in the Cinderella fairy tale, the appearance of the godmother at the crucial moment brings the situation to another level where transformation is possible and good can prevail. At this point in my dream the curtains are drawn back, and I enter the darkness. When I first looked for direction about what my gift or purpose in life might be, I had a dream where I was looking for a tape of the song *'Any Dream Will Do.'* The opening lines are, "I close my eyes, drew back the curtain to see for certain what I thought I knew." The song comes from *Joseph and the Amazing Technicolour Dreamcoat* and continues with the title phrase, 'any dream will do.' This was a usefully clear response to my quest for purpose in my life. The reference, of course, is to Joseph and his dream-work in the Scriptures.

As we have seen repeatedly in this book, be on the lookout for symbols that recur in your dreams. For me, the image in this song of 'drawing back the curtains' indicates opening up to what lies hidden or in darkness. I must be about 'My Father's Business' and follow the wisdom from this dream guidance, i.e. carry out my inner/spiritual work through the wisdom of the dream. Any dream will do!

When I go inside, I find darkness at first, as with any inner journey. In nature, the caterpillar goes into the darkness of the cocoon to emerge transformed into a butterfly. Such metamorphosis is also possible for us when we have the courage to enter into our own darkness and carry out the work required for our healing.

This dream shows me, using the literal words themselves, that when I 'Heal My Own Heart' I can give the Bread of Life to others. This principle is found at the core of the Christian message, as well as at the core of the psychotherapeutic process.

Finding the light switch showed me the work required inside, instead of outside. The light switches were covered over by whitewash, which is not only used to paint walls but also contains a purifying agent. The traditional whitewash from the days of my childhood was made from the entirely natural element of limestone, devoid of artificial chemicals and used also to keep natural spring wells clean and pure. I understood the dream to mean my connection (to my power to bring light to inner, dark places) was preserved, although hidden, until I was ready to make my inner journey.

Dream: Saying Farewell to Parents

I am saying goodbye to my parents. I go to them and kiss them goodbye. Other members of the family are present and the scene is emotional, but I know I have to go somewhere with someone, whom I seem to know in the dream.

Reflection: Scripture tells us, in the gospel of Luke, "I tell you the truth. Jesus said to them, no one who has left home or wife or brothers or parents or children for the sake of the kingdom of God will fail to receive many times as much in this age and, in the age to come, eternal life." We must bid farewell to father and mother, brothers and sisters in order to follow Christ. In other words, when we are ready to commit to someone or something new in our lives, we must be willing to let go of something else and make the commitment a priority.

Dream: In Search of Love

We are in a place where there is a workshop in progress. A man takes us down a path to a stone garden. The garden is full of all sorts of so-called healing stones, little ones. We are looking for a Rose Quartz and I ask if it is also known as the Love Stone. At some stage I go there again with this man and a woman who was not with us the first time. There is another man there now and it looks like the top of the grave with a sort of altar on it. I am not very comfortable but I enter into the banter and fun about the stones we are finding. On our return, there are lots of pigs eating lush vegetation on a hill slope. I struggle to get up the hill and ask someone who happens to be lying there for a helping hand, and it is no problem. I get the support I need by asking.

Reflection: Returning to the garden a second time, I find balance, as the feminine principle is now present. On the first visit, one man was there while a woman and man were there on my return. The use of stone to mark sacred sites is a universal tradition and some crystal and other gemstones have been used as healing tools. The Rose Quartz has been associated with the heart chakra and love. Here in Ireland we have many Standing Stones, or Dolmens, marking the burial place of our ancient Chieftains. Often a large, flat stone has been placed on top, forming an altar. You could say we are finding something precious, relating to healing and love from a past (our Celtic tradition) that has been buried.

Going back, as I am doing when I encounter the pigs, means looking at our past. In keeping with our ancient culture, we remember St Patrick was brought to Ireland to herd pigs on our hills and know that he brought Christianity to Ireland. He escaped from this slavery and went back to Britain, as you will remember from his dream referenced earlier in this book. It was in his dreams too that he heard the people of Ireland calling him. Fortunately for us, he took his dream seriously and returned to bring the Faith to them/us.

The biblical story of the Prodigal Son (Luke 15) also uses porcine imagery. "And he would willingly have filled his belly with the husks the pigs were eating" before deciding to return to what he had once left behind in the place of his father. This son also gets the support he needs by returning and asking for forgiveness. Struggling to get up the hill could symbolise life's difficulties and challenges.

Our dreams frequently invite us to rediscover the wisdom of what we once knew and abandoned or buried through ignorance, fear, hurt or pride. We are challenged to integrate our past instead of burying it. The workshop taking place suggests anew the opportunity to learn and experience some ancient ways of healing through crystals and loving.

In modern times, crystal healing has been promoted as well as ridiculed. Unknown to many people the clerical tradition whereby newly ordained priests kiss the ring of their bishop was originally designed to conduct, through the ring's stone, the natural energy of the earth, infusing that energy into the blessing.

Long before we were debating the merits of 'New Age' there was the 'Old Age' wisdom of our ancestors, who understood how to tap the natural resources of Mother Earth. Ancient seers discerned not only water sources but also the location of natural energy points, building their altars accordingly. Such energy points are the equivalent of the *chakra* system in the body. Crystals are natural conductors of this energy. Thus, the bishop on the church altar dispensing this all-important blessing to a priest embarking on his vocation also uses the crystal on his finger to conduct natural energies, in this way integrating old wisdom with Christian ritual.

******

Crow Woman

Before falling asleep I had been reading the magazine called *Kindred Spirit*. The edition had many articles on matters of Spirit and all sorts of healing techniques, stories and testimonies focusing on the evolutional shifts for our times.

Dream: Crow Woman

In my dream, I am perturbed by the experience of my encounter with my mother as she is so utterly different from the mother I knew. I meet her as a wild and free spirit all dressed in black. She has left my father and is with another man. In my dream, I am aware that I have already had this dream of her leaving dad, something she would never have done as she was devoted to him.

Not only has she left him, but she has taken on the children of her latest partner. Somehow I am expected to go with her/them, and I am not prepared for this choice I have to make. It is as if I am one of their children who has to choose which parent to be loyal to. I really miss my old mother.

I seem to remember or realise that I have not been 'giving back' or making contribution to her, and I feel bad. At this point, I somehow realise that this is a theme from another dream which has a similar feeling to it. I am struck by how ruthless my mother is. She is all dressed in black and very focused. As I look more closely, I notice she is so black in her dress and face, and I see her feet and I say to myself, "She is Crow Woman."

I do not seem to be able to reach her, and she has no qualms or guilt about having left dad. She has this new man, and she is so vibrant and changed and it is very evident she has moved on. I decide I will not choose one over the other and that I will go back to my old tiny flat where I can be independent.

I cannot find my car (another familiar theme in my dreams), so I am desperate to find a way to either get through to her or escape. Somehow I go to her new man/lover and try to explain my dilemma to him. He is so attractive, strong, young and masculine with a lean body and long hair down to his waist. He reminds me of a Native American Indian.

I realise why my mother has fallen for him as he pulls me into his embrace. It is as if I cannot resist his masculinity and even though I have no intention of being seduced, I feel powerless to resist his strong and gentle embrace. I realise my Crow Woman mother is looking through venetian blinds at us as we embrace. My mother and I look each other in the eyes. As I pull myself away he asks if and when he can see me again ... I say I don't know.

She is enraged. Suddenly, she is no longer in black and has somehow lost her Crow Woman power and has packed up and left without us. I jump into the nearest car/van I find to get a lift to my old flat as my car is still lost, and I notice I am in the company of my mother's sister (my God-mother) and friends. I tell them about my ordeal and how ungrounded my mother is and appeal to them to talk to her.

Reflection: Before I even wrote this dream down I felt compelled to Google Crow Woman, even though I was not familiar with her. The first thing I found under this title was the *Dream Time* magazine site.

Within this I found *Crow Woman a Dream Messenger* by Jayne Gackenbach.

So what is her message to me at this time?

The first thing I discover is that Jayne Gackenbach has just completed a book about Crow Woman. Here am I writing my book about Dream Wisdom and Crow Woman shows up in my dream!

The quandary of Crow Woman, who was from the Native Cree culture of Canada, was to find a balance between the two worlds she was caught between - her Cree culture and the Western culture which surrounded and dominated her life. The story is about how this remarkable woman was to find psychological health as well as spiritual transcendence. I could say that this has also been my life long search and deep desire.

Crow Woman has to cope with the extremes in Native communities. In her story, she speaks of the pattern of family, community obligations and support in the context of a larger culture which challenges individualism. Crow Woman, like me, became involved in individual and group work, and like her, I too became a counsellor. The core challenge for us all is to help our selves and others to recover from our conditioned histories and addictions. It takes a lot of courage to 'be different' in the native culture of our individual experiences, beliefs and practices.

When Crow Woman was diagnosed with cancer she turned away from the world of surgery, chemotherapy and radiation and turned to the 'Old Man' or Shaman for healing. The Shaman she turned to explained about the purpose and need for suffering in our lives saying, 'You can only teach from your own suffering.' For me this is an example of integration, and at the heart of her story, Crow Woman strived for understanding and integration of the extremes in life. We are all thrown into, and called to encounter, the full range of human experience during our short sojourn in this life. As Crow Woman rose above her suffering, both psychological and physical in the end, it was through deep self-awareness and not denial that made her the great teacher she became.

The message of Crow Woman continues after her death to fulfil the beliefs and sensitivities of the Cree - that dreams are the 'place' where one receives 'visits' from those who have died or passed on.

This brings me back to the question of what message Crow Woman has for me through the 'dream visit' from my mother.

There are a few recurrent themes in it, as already sensed and stated in my dream, one being my mother having left my father and the other the feeling that I have not 'given back' or 'pulled my weight' to use local expression! Both themes are reflected in the story of Crow Woman referring to the pattern of family and community obligations. There is also the dilemma of leaving her original Cree culture to survive in the modern Western culture.

In my mother's culture it was native thinking to attend to and sustain the needs of her man and family. There was little or no room for her spirit to be free or wild outside that culture. I believe my dream is challenging me to leave that system of behaviour in my own relationship at the time. In other words, the part of me that is/was like my mother is being outgrown as my dream shows me mother has outgrown her old behaviour.

The 'giving back' theme, I believe, is about the idea I was brought up with which was to contribute to the household as soon as I was in a position to earn my own money. My current belief is that I must give back to the universe that which has been given to me. I am now working on 'giving back' to the world (via this book) some of the wisdom I have been fortunate enough to receive through dreams. My dream also presents me with the responsibility of choice!

For me, choice means having to take a stand. My dream challenges me to look at my old ways, which are tempting to return to at this time! I could return to my safe 'contained' flat, where I could be independent. I note that my car, symbolising ego, is lost or not available to me!

The final part of the dream is most challenging, as I look into the eyes of my mother as Crow Woman whilst I am in the arms of her new lover. When I say, "I don't know" to his request to see me again she loses her power and leaves. I must say "Yes" to a new and more empowering way!

I believe this to be the transpersonal spirit of my mother in her new wisdom, with a powerful message for me to outgrow her old ways of being with the man she loved and for me to find my personal free spirit power. I must let go of "I don't know" and choose.

Finding myself in the company of my God-mother is a blessing! In fairy tales we know that God-mother heralds change in the story when she arrives. God-mothers, by ritual, are supposed to fill in for our birth mothers in the event of being needed. In this instance, I believe the mothering from my dream to come from a higher or spiritual plane via Crow Woman.

A Gift for Life

Readers will have noticed that I am careful not to offer _Interpretations_ but _Reflections_ of dreams. This is because dream wisdom, like all wisdom, proceeds by unveiling and only reveals itself through gentle and sensitive probing. Careful probing along the lines of the reflections we have seen in these pages allows for the glimpsing of emerging wisdom and guidance.

The word 'No' comes very early on in our lives. We learn to tuck away our primitive feelings into our unconscious and a kernel forms inside our ego-shell, the persona we need to survive. Until we integrate that kernel, we will struggle to find our place. When we can explore inside our shell, with the aid of Dream Wisdom, we can make great progress in the integration that is full maturity.

Dreams matter to all of us, from Nobel laureates to suckling infants, but our understanding can often be impaired by the authorities we have set up in our lives and hearts. It is all too easy to become alienated, whether by distractions or by a sort of blindness to the symbols our deeper Self offers up. Sometimes the message can be challenging or even seem flimsy, but as we have seen, even a snippet can be deeply revealing.

This book has been an attempt to look afresh at the language of dreams, and I trust it has left you with your inner eyes peeled for the symbols and images nightly presented. Dreams can seem ambiguous and irrational but Dream Wisdom is often very pointed and asks us to get to the essence, sometimes through even the use of puns that are obvious once we are tuned into them.

Dream guidance is something else! Because it comes from the Spirit, it is greater than our imagination, which usually comes from the conscious mind. The two together work like a dream.

The function of a dream, in a nutshell, is to warn, to challenge, to direct and to heal. Given this abundance, we do well to look at dreams as gifts crafted for us uniquely.

Prepare to be surprised. Breathe *in* the openness, breathe *out* the distractions and obstacles, and become aware of the journey. The Psyche is an amazing antenna and searches out anything it can bring back and use to arouse those dormant feelings in your heart.

> *I thank God for my dream life.*
> Amelia E. Barr

Appendices

Appendix 1

Nine Practical Suggestions to Access Your Dream Wisdom

Certain suggestions have been especially useful for clients and pupils seeking to remember their dreams. Here they are again, for handy reference:

1 Before going to sleep, offer an intention to be attentive to your waking.

2 When you wake, linger at the moment between sleeping and waking.

3 In a notebook kept beside your bed write down your dream exactly as you recall it paying attention to as much detail as you can.

4 At first, make no attempt to understand or analyse your dream.

5 Note in particular the opening scene or place where your dream takes place.

6 The final scene and especially the energy or feeling at the point where we wake up is most important to note.

7 Scan the day or days prior to the dream for clues as to what the dream is trying to help you with.

8 Try not to be selective about which dreams you write down.

9 Note patterns or repeated symbols in your dreams.

Appendix 2

Examples of dreams in the Bible

Abraham's dream vision - Genesis 15:12-21

Jacob's dream - Genesis 28:10-22

Dreams in the life of Joseph - Genesis 37:5-11; Ch.40-41.

Solomon's dream - 1 Kings 3:5-15

Samuel's call -1 Samuel 3:3-14

Eliphaz's dream - Job 4:12-21

Isiah's call - Isaiah 6:1-13

Ezekiel's visions - Ezekiel 1:1-3

Ezekiel's 'dry bones' vision - Ezekiel 37

Dreams in the life of Daniel - Daniel 2-4

Zachariah's vision Luke - 1:11-20

Joseph's dream Matthew - 1:20-21

Shepherd's vision - Luke 2:8-14

Joseph's other dreams - Matthew 2:13-21

Baptism of Jesus - Matthew 3:16-17

Transfiguration - Luke 9:28-36

Paul's conversion vision - Acts 9:3-9

Peter's dream vision - Acts 10:3-21

Paul's night visions - Acts 16:9; 18:9; 23:11; 27:23.

Appendix 3

Further Reading

Barton, Anthony. *Three Worlds of Therapy*
    (Palo Alto, 1974: National Press Books)

Boa, Fraser and von Franz, Marie-Louise. *The Way of the Dream*
    (Canada, 1988: Windrose)

Chetwynd, Tom. *Dictionary for Dreamers*
    (St Albans, 1977: Paladin)

Claremont de Castillejo, Irene. *Knowing Woman*
    (New York, 1973: Harper Colophon Books)

Cogley, Jim. *Wood You Believe Vol. 1: The Unfolding Self*
    (Wexford 2005: Cogley), *Wood You Believe Vol. 2: The*
    Emerging Self (Wexford 2005: Cogley), *Wood You Believe*
    Vol. 3: The Ancestral Self (Wexford 2007: Cogley), *Wood*
    You Believe Vol. 4: The Twinless Self
    (Wexford 2011: Cogley)

Ferrucci, Piero. *What We May Be: Techniques for Psychological*
    and Spiritual Growth Through Psychosynthesis
    (Los Angeles, 1982: Tarcher)

Goodison, Lucy. *Moving Heaven and Earth: Sexuality, Spirituality*
    and Social Change (London, 1992: HarperCollins
    Pandora), *In Our Own Hands: A Book of Self-Help Therapy*
    (London, 1981: Women's Press)

Gray, John. *Men are from Mars, Women are from Venus*
    (New York, 1992: HarperCollins)

Hayton, Althea. *A Silent Cry: Womb Twin Survivors Tell Their*
    Story (St Albans, 2008: Wren Publications), *Untwinned:*
    Perspectives on the Death of a Twin before Birth
    (St Albans, 2007: Wren Publications)

Hederman, Mark Patrick. *Walkabout: Life as Holy Spirit*
    (Dublin, 2005: Columba Press)

Jung, Carl G. *Memories, Dreams, Reflections* (New York, 1963:
    Pantheon), *Dreams*
    (Princeton, 1974: Princeton University Press)

Kaplan-Williams, Strephon. *The Dreamwork Manual: a Step-by-Step Introduction to Working with Dreams* (Wellingborough, 1991: Aquarian)

Kelsey, Morton. *Dreams: The Dark Speech of the Spirit* (New York, 1968: Doubleday), *Dreams: A Way to Listen to God* (New Jersey, 1978: Paulist Press)

O'Donohue, John. *Beauty: The Invisible Embrace* (New York, 2005: HarperCollins)

Ritchie, George. *Ordered To Return* (Newburyport, 1998: Hampton Roads)

Rubini, Constance and Frederic Bodet. *The Little Book of Miró* (Paris, 2005: Flammarion)

Savary, Louis and Patricia H. Berne and Strephon Kaplan Williams. *Dreams and Spiritual Growth: A Judeo-Christian Way of Dreamwork* (New Jersey, 1984: Paulist Press)

Skonieczna, Katarzyna. "Tony O'Malley and his 'green universe.'" *Terra Incognita*, 2008, www.tinyurl.com/c6k3xs8

Welch, John, *Spiritual Pilgrims: Carl Jung and Teresa of Avila* (New York, 1982: Paulist Press)

Woodman, Marion. *The Pregnant Virgin* (Toronto, 1997: Inner City Books)

Acknowledgments

To my family, who have been a constant source of presence, love and acceptance in my life, I am deeply grateful.

To my many clients, friends and faithful participants of workshops who have literally offered thousands of dreams to be explored, I am eternally grateful.

The late author and poet John O'Donohue was adamant in his encouragement that I should commit my dream talks and insights to paper. With his insistent challenge, I finally made a start. Heartfelt gratitude to my beloved John.

To Mary Fitzpatrick and Fr JJ Cribbin, for spiritual counsel in my youth, and Fr Benny McHale developed my love for Scripture.

To my wonderful circle of 'Thursday evening' friends - Ca Devine-McHale, Eva Brady, Ger Boyle, Beth Moran and Mary Quinn - your constant encouragement and urging have been so necessary to get me out of my rut of self-doubt.

Thanks to Ger Murphy and the late Úna Maguire from the Creative Counselling Centre.

Deep appreciation to Ed Boyne, Janet Murray and their students at the Tivoli Institute for trusting me with the privileged task of working with them.

Thanks to Terence McKeon, Deborah O'Neill Fearon, Suzanne Ellis (manuscript 'hawk-eye'), Angela Burt, Liamy Mac Nally, Barbara Robitaille, Craig Stewart, Angela Jennejahn, Cas McCarthy, Carol Williams and Fin Keegan of SixPens.com.

© Kathleen Duffy 2014